PRAISE FOR
SCORPIONS AND TURTLES

"Timeless, insightful best-selling authors Carnegie & Covey cracked the door open to show us key behaviors different people demonstrate, and now Dr. Singer has blown the doors off the hinges! His *SCORPIONS AND TURTLES* book breaks down how to survive our troubling times in ways everyone can understand and put into use right now in their own life."

—**Libby Craddock**
healthcare executive

"Scorpions beware! Dr. Bill Singer has written a book that uncovers the idiosyncrasies of your personality and behavior. Not only is it easy to understand as it is written with laypeople in mind, but the format is intriguing as it sets up scenarios and asks a series of questions illuminating your responses. As if that is not enough, the narrative provides comfort through nestled spiritual guidance. Thoroughly therapeutic and enlightening!"

—**Karen Silliter**, M.H.S.A.
compliance professional

"Dr. Singer offers practical suggestions for better mental and emotional health based on real-life experiences—a wealth of wisdom that would be helpful to anyone!"

—**Reverend Chuck Carlson**, B.S., M.DIV.
pastoral counselor and hospital chaplain

"Dr. Bill Singer has really opened my eyes. I cannot help but see "Scorpions" and "Turtles" everywhere I look, whether at work or in my personal life. I am AWAKE now, and I will NOT go back to sleepwalking. If you are an individual perplexed at why your life is so challenging, disappointing, or full of drama, *SCORPIONS AND TURTLES How To Survive Our Troubling Times* is a must-read!

Dr. Singer provides great insight into the challenges we all face in our everyday encounters with others by applying wisdom & insight on dominant behaviors illustrated in the fable of the scorpion and turtle. This seemingly amusing and straightforward illustration serves as an introduction to the "Foundational Human Knowledge" of love, loss, conflict, leadership, and many others. I learned how they impact our relationships and self-image.

Key to the reader, such as myself, are the tools in the *SCORPIONS AND TURTLES Coaching Companion Workbook*. It helped me understand myself better, and understand how I interact with others. It is of greatest importance to me because it encouraged and guided me. I transformed into my best self as I learned how to use each of the foundational human knowledge areas which will help me survive our troubling times."

—**Sharon Mullins**, M.A., B.S.N., R.N.
clinical improvement nurse leader

SCORPIONS AND TURTLES

How To Survive Our Troubling Times

SCORPIONS AND TURTLES

How To Survive Our Troubling Times

DR. BILL HALEVI SINGER,
Psy.D., M.S.W., L.C.S.W., C.A.P.

Copyright © 2025 Dr. Bill Halevi Singer. All rights reserved.

It is illegal to reproduce, duplicate, or transmit any part of this document through any means, including electronic and printed formats. Recording of this publication is strictly prohibited without the express written permission of the publisher, exception in the case of a brief quotation in a book review.

The author of this workbook does not intend you to take this as medical advice or as a prescription or a form of treatment for physical, mental, emotional, or medical problems, without the advice of a physician or licensed mental health professional. The intent of the author is only to offer information to help you in your quest for emotional and spiritual well-being. In the event you use any of the information in this book on your own, the author does not assume responsibility for your actions.

Publisher: Singer Institute LLC Orlando, Florida (USA)
Illustrations & Tools: Diane Newton (USA)
Editing: Nina Shoroplova (Canada) and Franklin Obi (Nigeria)
Cover Design: Pagatana Design Service (Indonesia)
Book Interior and e-book Design: Amit Dey (India)
Production & Publishing, Pagatana Design Service (Indonesia)
Consultant: Geoff Affleck (Canada)
Graphics Design: Heather Wight (England)

ISBN 978-1-7355590-2-5 (hardback)
ISBN 978-1-7355590-0-1 (paperback)
ISBN 978-1-7355590-1-8 (ebook)

Library of Congress Number 2020923445

SEL021000 SELF-HELP / Motivational & Inspirational
SEL027000 SELF-HELP / Personal Growth / Happiness
SEL032000 SELF-HELP / Spiritual
PSY031000 PSYCHOLOGY / Social Psychology
PSY007000 PSYCHOLOGY / Clinical Psychology

SCORPIONS AND TURTLES
WORKBOOKS, JOURNALS, VIRTUAL GROUPS & COURSES

Dr. Bill Singer offers you four ways to integrate the contents of the SCORPIONS AND TURTLES How To Survive Our Troubling Times book* into your life:

1. Coaching Companion Workbook**
2. Personal Workbooks** & Journals (#1-#13)**
3. Virtual Groups (#1-13)
4. Courses

Available in:
* - Paperback, ebook, & audiobook
** - Paperback & ebook

Order at SingerInstitute.com
or scan QR code

SCORPIONS AND TURTLES
HOW TO SURVIVE OUR TROUBLING TIMES
PERSONAL WORKBOOKS*
& JOURNALS*

#1—Intention, Trust, Motivation & Disappointment
#2—Survival, Love, Fear & Living
#3—Addiction, Loss, Grief & Dying
#4—Expectations, Beliefs, Communication & Habits
#5—Change, Independence, Insight & Awareness
#6—Present, Past, Future & Situations
#7—Denial, Truth, Learning & Justification
#8—Doing, Instincts, Passivity & Empathy
#9—Free Will, Emotion, Hate & Human Footprint
#10—Cooperation, Magical Thinking, Commitment & Attachment
#11—Thinking, Human Brain, Focus & Human Evolution
#12—Interdependence, Dependence, Impulse Control & Self-Acceptance
#13—Talent, Leadership, Conflict & Competition

Available in:
* - Paperback & ebook

Order at SingerInstitute.com
or scan QR code

SCORPIONS AND TURTLES
HOW TO SURVIVE OUR TROUBLING TIMES
VIRTUAL GROUPS

For maximum benefit, let me encourage you to participate in all of the virtual groups that I have created to enhance your personal growth and development so you can do life better! All virtual groups are provided on-demand for your viewing convenience. Each virtual group covers four different foundational human knowledge areas.

#1—Intention, Trust, Motivation & Disappointment
#2—Survival, Love, Fear & Living
#3—Addiction, Loss, Grief & Dying
#4—Expectations, Beliefs, Communication & Habits
#5—Change, Independence, Insight & Awareness
#6—Present, Past, Future & Situations
#7—Denial, Truth, Learning & Justification
#8—Doing, Instincts, Passivity & Empathy
#9—Free Will, Emotion, Hate & Human Footprint
#10—Cooperation, Magical Thinking, Commitment & Attachment
#11—Thinking, Human Brain, Focus & Human Evolution
#12—Interdependence, Dependence, Impulse Control & Self-Acceptance
#13—Talent, Leadership, Conflict & Competition

Join virtual groups at SingerInstitute.com or scan QR Code

SCORPIONS AND TURTLES
HOW TO SURVIVE OUR TROUBLING TIMES
COURSES

SCORPIONS AND TURTLES FULL COURSE includes:

- Original *SCORPIONS AND TURTLES book**
- *SCORPIONS AND TURTLES Coaching Companion Workbook***
- <u>All</u> 13 *SCORPIONS AND TURTLES Personal Workbooks*** *& Journals***
- Access to all 13 *SCORPIONS AND TURTLES Virtual Groups*

SCORPIONS AND TURTLES MINI COURSE includes:

- Original *SCORPIONS AND TURTLES book**
- *SCORPIONS AND TURTLES Coaching Companion Workbook***
- One *SCORPIONS AND TURTLES Personal Workbook*** *& Journal*** (Choose from the workbook titles #1 - 13 and the corresponding Personal Journal)
- One corresponding *SCORPIONS AND TURTLES Virtual Group*

Available in:
* - Paperback, ebook, & audiobook
** - Paperback & ebook

**Register at SingerInstitute.com
or scan QR Code**

DEDICATION

I dedicate this workbook to all the first responders and various individuals and groups across the world who take the risk of offering help to those in need for the betterment of this world and who protect us from those who would seek to destroy humankind. Their acts of courage and kindness show the world who they are. You are truly heroes and my inspiration!

CONTENTS

Special Thanks xv
Author's Note xvii
Introduction xix

Part I Ancient Fables 1

    Chapter One: The Fable of the Scorpion and the Turtle 3

    Chapter Two: Let Us Go Deeper 9

    Chapter Three: How People with Scorpion-Like Behaviors Are Born 13

    Chapter Four: How People with Scorpion-Like Behaviors Are Made 17

Part II Foundational Human Knowledge 23

    Chapter Five: Is It Just Sibling Rivalry? 27

    Chapter Six: Love Finds a Way 47

    Chapter Seven: Addiction and Relationships Don't Mix 61

    Chapter Eight: It's Never Enough 77

    Chapter Nine: What About Me? 93

Chapter Ten: Good Decision or Not? 107

Chapter Eleven: It's a Secret 123

Chapter Twelve: It's All About the Money. 139

Chapter Thirteen: A One-Way Ticket 155

Chapter Fourteen: Death and Divorce 171

Chapter Fifteen: Very Special Indeed 191

Chapter Sixteen: Finding Your Way 211

Chapter Seventeen: Welcome to the Real World. 227

Part III Your Best Life. 247

Chapter Eighteen: Taking Responsibility for Your Life 251

Chapter Nineteen: Reality Check 255

Chapter Twenty: Real-World Reality versus Virtual-World Reality. 257

Chapter Twenty-One: A Brief Message to Turtle-Like People . . 265

Chapter Twenty-Two: A Brief Message to Scorpion-Like People. . 267

Chapter Twenty-Three: Bonus: Being versus Doing 271

Epilogue. 275

Acknowledgments 285

About the Author 287

Appendices 289

    Glossary of Definitions of Each Foundational Human Knowledge 289

    Chapter Review Plans 299

    Foundatinal Human Knowledge List 305

SPECIAL THANKS

To my mom, Peggy Ann, who gave much of her life energy to ensure I discovered who I was destined to be. Even though I know she did all she could to be here with me to see this book through to publishing, what is most important is that her life struggles are over, and she is now with the Prince of Peace!

AUTHOR'S NOTE

I believe we will be judged by future generations, not just on how technologically advanced we were or how much we knew of the world, but by how we treated those who were most in need among us.

I also believe in both giving back and paying it forward. With that in mind, I intend on giving a portion of the sales of this book to be used for the enhancement of the human condition, this planet, and in support of people who are trying to help others reach their potential.

Dr. Bill Halevi Singer

INTRODUCTION

Please take a deep breath and release it slowly. Now, I believe you are better prepared to answer an essential question. Can you say with absolute certainty what knowledge is critical for you to acquire and know in this world? Many years ago, Socrates took "To know thyself," which was inscribed on the Temple of Delphi. He adopted it as the most important knowledge.[1]

If this statement is true, then I am proposing the second most important knowledge you need to know and understand concerns people with scorpion-like behaviors and people with turtle-like behaviors, and what they can teach you. This unique self-improvement book will include stories of people with scorpion-like behaviors, people with turtle-like behaviors, and foundational human knowledge to help you understand more about yourself and all human beings. I hope you will agree with me that, no matter how much you know, it is probably not enough because there is always room for learning more.

I have discovered that one of the major challenges of being human is that none of us was born "knowing"; we must learn everything! There are many self-improvement and survival books out there for you to choose from. The real challenge is determining what information is most useful to help you survive our troubling times.

---

[1] LeDoux J, Brown R, Pine D, Hofmann S. Know Thyself: Well-Being and Subjective Experience. Cerebrum. 2018 Jan 1;2018:cer-01-18. PMID: 30746034; PMCID: PMC6353121.

This self-improvement book intends to provide you with critical knowledge, insight, encouragement, and wisdom to help you survive our troubling times. I will try to bring you closer to your human potential and help you experience what it is like to win more in life and do it better. This book is designed to be interactive, and you will receive maximum benefit if you choose to participate actively. Our journey together will begin by offering you a better understanding of people by using an ancient fable, followed in Part II by my giving you the opportunity to learn what I will refer to as "*Foundational Human Knowledge.*"

> I define Foundational Human Knowledge as knowledge that is universal, timeless, and essential to human existence and survival.

You may want to think of this type of knowledge as a well-built foundation for a house. You know that every solid house or building has a foundation upon which it stands. This foundation might not be visible, but it is always present to support such a building. **A foundation affects all aspects of everything built upon it for the life of the building or that for which it supports. If the foundation is not strong and right, the structure or that which is built upon it will never be strong and right. Hence, it is the same with all foundations and everything built upon them. I refer to this as the** *Law of Foundations*.

As foundations are with every structure, so they are with every human life. Every human life begins with a foundation of human knowledge. To that end, I intend to share with you fifty-two essential foundational human knowledge terms. Once learned and put into practice, the foundational human knowledge terms that I share will help you build a strong foundation for your future. This foundation will help you avoid unnecessary pain and show you how to survive and thrive throughout your life. Let us get started!

Part I
Ancient Fables

CHAPTER ONE

THE FABLE OF THE SCORPION AND THE TURTLE

A long time ago, in a faraway place, the scorpion found itself in great need. It traveled far, was fatigued to the point of needing to rest, and was stuck at the edge of a fast-flowing river. The scorpion could not proceed with its journey until it found a way to cross the river safely. Faced with the dilemma of not accomplishing its goals, the scorpion quickly became frustrated and exasperated. The scorpion thought long and hard to itself. "What can I do? I can't turn around and go back to where I came from, and I can't think of any other options."

After being at the edge of the river for a while, the scorpion noticed something coming from afar. Initially, it could not make out what it was because it was so far away. As it came closer and closer, the scorpion could see it was a large turtle. At this point, the sun was getting hotter and hotter, and the scorpion was getting more concerned about its situation.

When the scorpion thought the turtle was close enough to hear, it shouted across the river, "Hi, there, fellow traveler, I have been here for some time waiting for assistance."

The turtle had good eyesight, was cautious, and had kept its distance from the scorpion, which was why the scorpion had to shout to the turtle from so far away.

The turtle responded to the scorpion with a question. "How can I assist you?"

The scorpion replied, "I have been traveling for a long time, and I must reach my destination soon. However, I discovered this river in front of me. Being a poor swimmer, I could not cross it. I was wondering if you could help me by giving me a ride across the river on your back. I know that you are a young, strong, good, and experienced swimming turtle in your prime."

The turtle responded: "I may be rather young and a good swimmer, but I was not born yesterday! You are a scorpion, and if I agree to take you across the river, surely at some point, you will sting me, and I will sustain fatal wounds."

The scorpion responded with, "Oh, no, my new turtle friend. I would never do that to you! That is not what friends do to friends. Besides, I cannot swim very well, and if something happened to you, it would happen to me too. What would be the logic in that?"

The turtle gave that thought and saw no flaw in the logic, so being a kind soul, said, "You are right. That would not be very logical, would it?" The turtle showed its trust in the scorpion by getting closer and closer until finally, when it was close enough, it stopped and said, "Go ahead and get on my back. I will take you across the river, my new friend. I could never live with myself if you tried to cross the river on your own and something bad happened to you."

"You are most kind," said the scorpion while it slowly crawled onto the turtle's back.

The river was fuller than usual due to the recent heavy rains, and the current was strong. As the turtle entered the water, it said to the scorpion, "Hang on my friend, I will take you across this treacherous river safely."

"Okay, thank you. I will hang on tight as if my very life depended on it," the scorpion said.

The turtle and the scorpion began to cross the river. It took a great deal of effort for the turtle. The turtle did not give up throughout the ordeal. As the turtle was touching the bank on the other side of the river, the scorpion positioned its tail with its large venomous barb full of poison and, without any hesitation, thrust it into an unprotected area of the turtle's body. The trusting turtle was shocked and stunned by what had just happened! The turtle thought to itself, "How could a friend do this to me?"

The scorpion got off the turtle's back and stepped on to the riverbank's dry land. With its last bit of life energy, the turtle asked the scorpion, "Why would you do this to me? I thought we were friends, and you promised me you would never hurt me."

The scorpion had a puzzled look on its face, smirked, and said, **"I am a scorpion and that is what scorpions do!"**

Origin of the Fable

It was impossible for me to track down a copy of the original fable. Therefore, I compiled the essence of the fable from many sources and presented it in a more modern form for you, the reader. However, I did find its origin. It seems to come from a collection of fables and is likely Persian in origin.[2]

---

[2] The Anvár-i Suhailí; Or, the Lights of Canopus; Being the Persian Version of the Fables of Pilpay; Or the Book "Kalílah and Damnah," Rendered Into Persian by Ḥusain Vá'izḥ U'l-Káshifí: Literally Translated Into Prose and Verse by Edward B. Eastwick. (n.d.-b). Google Books.

A Similar Fable

Some time ago, another fable surfaced that was like the original fable. I will present you with an abbreviated version since you are familiar with the original fable. I have added my artistic touch to it. I think it confirms just how behavior is universal, no matter where you live in the world.

It all started in Russia, where a wise man observed something quite extraordinary. Subsequently, he spoke to his clan about it several times a year until it became a well-known fable across the land. It is the fable of *The Scorpion and the Frog*.[3]

This Russian fable is like the original scorpion and turtle fable with a few important changes. It goes something like this: a Russian frog was playing and swimming along the side of a river. The frog had been on land for a while but decided to take a dip to cool off because it was a hot and humid day. As the frog was swimming without minding what was happening around it, there came a noise from the land that it could not ignore.

The frog looked up from the water and saw the scorpion lying on a rock. The scorpion did not look too well and was clearly in need of water. As the frog was looking, the scorpion said, "Hi, there. Could you spare a little water for a thirsty traveler?" The frog said, "Who? Me?" "Yes," said the scorpion.

The frog had never seen a scorpion before and had always been hospitable and kind to others. The frog came closer and pushed a leaf with some water over to the traveler, who reached down and drank. The scorpion said, "That was good. Can I have some more, please?"

---

[3] AesopFables.com - The Scorpion and the Frog - General Fable collection. (n.d.). http://aesopfables.com/cgi/aesop1.cgi?srch&fabl/TheScorpionandtheFrog.

The frog said, "Sure," and pushed over another leaf with some water until the scorpion had its fill.

After a few moments, the scorpion asked the frog for a ride over to the other side of the river because it could not swim. The frog, who had already helped the scorpion, said to itself, "Why not?" Then it said, "Okay" to the scorpion.

The scorpion gently climbed onto the frog's back, and they set out for the other side of the river.

They were two-thirds of the way there when the scorpion stung the frog on the back. The frog was shocked and surprised by the sharp pain it felt from the sting and asked, "Why did you do this to yourself and me since you can't swim? I am sure you will not be able to make it across to the other side of the river on your own."

The scorpion said, "I am a scorpion and that is who I am, and I have no choice. It's in my nature!"

Then, they both sank to the bottom of the river, never to be seen or heard from again.

Conventional wisdom from the two fables would lead us to believe that turtles and frogs are too trusting and somewhat naïve. On the other hand, scorpions only think of themselves. They do not care whether they hurt others or even themselves to get what they want. All turtles and scorpions are born the way they are, and they cannot change, no matter what happens in their lives.

CHAPTER TWO

LET US GO DEEPER

Now that you know the original ancient fable of the scorpion and the turtle, and a variation of the fable, you may be asking yourself, "Dr. Bill, why do I need to pay attention to these ancient fables?" I can quickly come up with at least three valid reasons.

1. Human beings share much in common with other animals across this planet.
2. The future of humankind is at a tipping point.
3. I believe your very survival and the survival of this planet may depend on what wisdom you learn from the fable of the scorpion and the turtle.

Important Understanding from These Ancient Fables

I know how easy it would be to come to a common finite set of conclusions concerning the fables and stop there. I would urge you to do what is necessary to give yourself the opportunity in this evergreen self-improvement book to gain much more understanding. I believe you will discover that some things, which usually appear obvious, may not provide the full explanation. You must go deeper if you want to find the truth. My goal is for you to apply this new knowledge to the "human" part of being a human being.

In Part II of this self-improvement book, I will introduce you to life-changing, Foundational Human Knowledge and how knowing it can profoundly affect your life. I challenge you to take the time you need to learn from what I am offering to you. I believe you must understand all you can from these ancient fables, stories, and the foundational human knowledge presented. Here are some reasons why it is vital for you to prepare yourself psychologically and emotionally for the real probability of certain life events, that are natural and unnatural. Every day, people are facing the potential challenges of famines. droughts, floods, wildfires, volcanoes, earthquakes, tornadoes, hurricanes, the collapse of the global financial system, including the crash of the United States Stock Market, rumors of wars, and wars including World War III and beyond.

Essential Knowledge

I want to give you a heads-up. Given what is happening in this world with both human made and natural disasters on the rise, you will need all of the essential knowledge and wisdom contained in this book to survive and thrive this new world reality and reset. It is time to examine the connections between the scorpion and turtle fable and human beings. You are going to have to use your imagination or at least follow mine very soon. So, get ready.

It has been my privilege over a lifetime to meet many people. It is not too much of a stretch for me to imagine people as scorpions, turtles, or even a side of a coin. You may know that government-made coins usually have a head side and a tail side. I can picture in my mind turtles as the head side and scorpions as the tail side. If I think about the fables and coins, I can see certain things all humans have in common with both.

For instance, when a person is operating like a turtle, I see the person displaying the characteristics of a coin's head side.

On the other hand, if the person is functioning like a scorpion, I see them displaying the characteristics of the tail side of a coin. You might be aware that you have a 50 percent chance to land heads and a 50 percent chance that it will land tails when you flip a coin a hundred times. It is easier to accept these chances when a coin is tossed if one understands that the coin operates under the Laws of Large Numbers.[4]

My professional experience has taught me that human beings are like tossed coins that operate under specific laws of their own. Even if the laws are not yet fully known or understood, it does not imply they do not exist. To some degree, I believe each of us has options, whether to operate as a person with turtle-like behaviors or a person with scorpion-like behaviors, within the context of the law of foundations and other factors. I think this could explain why some people are turtle-like while others are scorpion-like during their lives.

It is my observation that most people are born more turtle-like. However, some individuals may adopt scorpion-like people's thinking and behavioral patterns. This adaptation may occur because of many factors like age, brain wiring, amount and frequency of hurt and pain, tolerance, the intensity of trauma, personality types, resiliency factors, aptitude, life learning experiences or lack thereof, cultural influences, genes, and other biological factors, while operating under universal laws at the same time.

---

[4] Gut, A., & Gut, A. (2005). Probability: a graduate course (Vol. 200, No. 5). New York: Springer.

Thus far, I have attempted to stretch your imagination, challenge your thinking, and raise your awareness to the following truth: we human beings are a part of a larger worldwide ecosystem, operating under specific foundational laws, known and unknown, and within humanity is an ecosystem exhibiting scorpion-like and turtle-like behaviors. There is much more! Now, it is time to go deeper still.

CHAPTER THREE

HOW PEOPLE WITH SCORPION-LIKE BEHAVIORS ARE BORN

In this section, I will share my thoughts on what makes a person have scorpion-like behaviors from birth. Please note that some of what I will explain to you is not "hard science"[5], but comes directly from decades of personal and professional experience.

You may recall from a human biology class you had in school that a natural fifty-fifty ratio of males to females is born if nature is not altered artificially; and that usually, certain human body parts and characteristics develop before others over the given period of nine months, before one is born.[6] This includes our brain, talents, aptitude, potential muscle mass, height, weight, skin color, and temperament, which is tied to our frustration tolerance, personality, and other inherent personal characteristics. I believe all of these attributes are directly connected to our purpose.

---

[5] https://www.dictionary.com/browse/hard-science.
[6] Chao, F., Gerland, P., Cook, A. R., & Alkema, L. (2019). Systematic assessment of the sex ratio at birth for all countries and estimation of national imbalances and regional reference levels. Proceedings of the National Academy of Sciences of the United States of America, 116(19), 9303–9311. https://doi.org/10.1073/pnas.1812593116.

Yes, I know we exist for a purpose, just like every other created thing. Our purpose makes each one of us special, and it is the reason we are created in the first place. I believe what each of us is given at birth makes us unique, and this uniqueness is our human potential. You may also be aware that we receive part of our biological attributes from past generations in addition to who we are.

People with scorpion-like behaviors are strongly tied to the past, as we all are to some degree due to our genetics. It seems people with scorpion-like behaviors are partly born as a result of previous generations who passed on their dominant genes. Over thousands of years, those genes became more and more dominant due to an ever-increasingly abusive environment centered around how to survive. Many of these survival challenges exist today, even if their type and form have changed. **It makes sense to me that the brain of a human born more scorpion-like has been designed with much of what they require to fight for what they need to survive, no matter the odds.** This is not judgment or condemnation on my part; rather, it is an observation.

This adaptation process by all life forms makes future generations more prepared to succeed than previous generations. This is a natural process designed to keep the total species from going into extinction. This changes their gene pool. This is not just speculation on my part. Science discerns that one generation's environment affects the genes passed on to the next generation.

You may know that if a child is born a boy, they get one X chromosome from the mother and a Y chromosome from the father. Likewise, when a girl child is born, the two X chromosomes come one from the father and one from the mother. Males have an

X and a Y chromosome, and females have two X chromosomes.[7] I learned early in my career that human beings receive their temperament at birth, defined as our inborn combination of mental, emotional, and character traits, which are seen as the valued aspects of a person's behavior.[8] It was only recently confirmed that the temperament we are born with stays with us throughout our lifetime.[9]

As I stated before, we are made up of genes from all generations in our bloodline, and we are ultimately an aggregate of genes from all previous generations of our species. These genes can be dominant or recessive. If they are dominant, they will be passed on to the next generation and so on.[10]

Sometimes, we do not fully understand that this transfer of genetic information from one generation to another is not the only thing happening.

Still with me? I hope so.

Now, let us focus on understanding people who have scorpion-like behaviors. I will describe the typical character traits of some people with scorpion-like behaviors using well-known adjectives. Due to their unique biological formation, people with scorpion-like behaviors are predisposed to behave similarly. They can be jealous, impatient, unfaithful, selfish, manipulative, unloving, and amoral. They may see themselves as being above the rules. They can be high achievers, are into power and control, and are often presented as leaders to others. They will always have

---

[7] Genetics Home Reference (GHR). (2020, 2 11). Y Chromosome. Retrieved from National Library of Medicine (NLM): https://ghr.nlm.nih.gov/chromosome/Y.

[8] childdevelopmentinfo.com/child-development/temperament_and_your_child/#gs.3ev0l8.

[9] courses.lumenlearning.com/suny-lifespandevelopment2/chapter/temperament/.

[10] Sayres, M. A., Lohmueller, K. E., Lohmueller, K. E., & Nielsen, R. (2014). Natural selection reduced diversity on human Y chromosomes. PLOS Genetics, 10(1). Retrieved 2 16, 2020, from https://journals.plos.org/plosgenetics/article?id=10.1371/journal.pgen.1004064.

a central goal and often seek power to ultimately control others and their surroundings to obtain their goals at all costs. Some people may see them as narcissists or psychopaths,[11] while others may see them as damaged people. That may be the case for some of them, but as you know, it is never as simple as it looks.

I intend to give you some critical insight into what to look for to help you identify and understand them better. If you want to know if someone is scorpion-like, observe how they deal with the word "no." It has been my experience that they do not deal well with it. You will want to make sure you are safe in all ways when you find out. People with scorpion-like behaviors have a common way of ultimately dealing with a perceived, permanent "no." They will most likely become angry because they have low frustration tolerance. They will often use threats and can move quickly to physical force or other means of aggression if cornered or made to solve their problems right away. At times, they may become passive until it is time to place the final, fatal sting.

In the next chapter, I will examine other considerations that personality and social psychologists generally agree must be reviewed when looking at the reasons for human behavior.[12]

---

[11] James SW. The criminal personality as a DSM-III-R antisocial, narcissistic, borderline, and histrionic personality disorder. Int J Offender Ther Comp Criminol. 1988;32:185–99. [Google Scholar]

[12] Donald W. Fiske (1994) Two Cheers for the Big Five!, Psychological Inquiry, 5:2, 123-124, DOI: 10.1207/s15327965pli0502_5.

CHAPTER FOUR

HOW PEOPLE WITH SCORPION-LIKE BEHAVIORS ARE MADE

Previously, I described genetics' role and how a person is predisposed to a range of behavioral possibilities and potential default programs, given the perceived need of the person's brain to survive.

Now, I would like to turn your attention to how people with scorpion-like behaviors may be made as a result of environmental factors. In response to the environment, a scorpion-like person will most likely be prompted subconsciously (based on the instinct to survive) and then consciously (based on getting what the person wants at all costs).

In my practice, I sometimes find it helpful to explain and help people understand why the people in their lives might do what they do. Often, scorpion-like people's behavior often comes from what they have learned from their caregivers, friends, and their direct experiences in the world.

I have found that many adults with scorpion-like behaviors have either been hurt by others physically or emotionally. As a result, they have adopted certain beliefs, attitudes, and actions. They are always in survival mode, consciously or subconsciously.

I have worked with many children and adults who have been significantly hurt physically and deeply wounded emotionally by others. From my experience, the following is my best explanations as to why people who are hurt and have not gone through the healing process tend to hurt others.

We all know human beings must learn to survive. Because of this, what one has learned is what one will use to survive in the future. Said another way, people only know what they know. It would be unreasonable to expect someone who has been hurt deeply and has not done the work to heal not to hurt others because that is what they know. To survive, scorpion-like people become very adaptive. That is why they will often act like a rubber band. *Rubber band,* you say. Yes, a rubber band will stretch if it needs to, but it will take its original form as soon as it no longer must. As it is with rubber bands, so it is with most people who possess scorpion-like behaviors. People with scorpion-like behaviors may seem to be changed if they are stopped for a while or decide it is in their best interest to "play the game." However, given enough time, if not transformed, they will always return to their natural scorpion-like form in the end.

Quite early in their lives and throughout adult-hood, scorpion-like people learn from other scorpion-like people how to get what they want from

> **As it is with rubber bands, so it is with most people who possess scorpion-like behaviors.**
>
> **People with scorpion-like behaviors may seem to be changed if they are stopped for a while or decide it is in their best interest to "play the game." However, given enough time, if not transformed, they will always return to their natural scorpion-like form in the end.**

others. There are a lot of intelligent people with scorpion-like behaviors. Most of them have received positive received positive reinforcement from years of toxic exposure to world messages such as, "Life is all about getting what you want, regardless of what it does to others in this world." They learned that to survive, they must take what they want from others; nobody truly cares about them, so why should they care about others or this world? Life becomes only about them, and if they are to obtain what they want in life, they must go out there and do whatever it takes to get it.

There are some people with scorpion-like behaviors for whom want and need become plain greed. There is never enough, so they must get theirs and yours as they try in vain to satisfy themselves. They have adopted the belief that "the ends justify the means."

People with scorpion-like behaviors are very persuasive because they often believe what they are saying and doing is right. That does not absolve intentional, selfish manipulation, which is inherent in a person with scorpion-like behavior. It would not be uncommon for people to hear me say, "I believe someone did the best they could at the time." I know that is not easy to hear for some people or believe when the other person is in scorpion-like mode and harms others or themselves.

I have discovered that many people with scorpion-like behaviors do not always intend to hurt others by being themselves. People with scorpion-like behaviors are master manipulators and have convinced themselves of the rightness of their beliefs. They often lie about anything. It does not matter if it is a big or a little thing.

They choose to live by a false belief that perception equals reality. Because they must survive, their reality is the only reality that matters. This is just one of many things that do not make sense to most people in a relationship with them. I often hear from someone in the life of a scorpion-like person that they lie all the time, even when they do not have to. I also realize some people with scorpion-like behaviors lie because there is little truth in them. In some cases, truth does not exist at all.

Today's world seems to be a society of judgment and retribution. I have observed many human beings have an unquenchable thirst for a pound of flesh when they are wronged. I see this more often while working with couples when there is perceived or unmistakable evidence that one member violated the couple's agreement in some meaningful way. Their desire for a pound of flesh is evident in whoever believes they have been wronged, changing from loving to not. This indicates they want the other person who wronged them to feel as much pain as possible.

I find this interesting because when a person is hurt, it is clear they do not want to remain in pain, and they find the pain undesirable. Nonetheless, the person who has been hurt seems to feel they are justified to inflict as much pain as possible on the other person they previously cared about, so they can somehow feel better as a result. If this scorpion-like logic is hard for you to follow, then you are not alone.

This chapter has revealed a great deal of information about how people with scorpion-like behaviors are made, and their general characteristics, to provide you with the opportunity for greater understanding. I will now add more in this summary about what to look out for to help you avoid being hurt if you are a turtle-like person.

To survive, people with turtle-like behaviors must learn all they can about people with scorpion-like behaviors. They need to know it will likely be necessary to always protect themselves by better understanding and learning the foundational human knowledge offered in this book. This will help them survive and ultimately thrive in this world, primarily operated by scorpion-like people.

As you know, not all scorpion stings are fatal. People with scorpion-like behaviors can be fun and exciting to be around if you do not get in their way. Never make the mistake of underestimating them and believing they will ultimately put your interest above theirs. I have seen so many marriages ruined and lives shattered because a person with turtle-like behaviors put their full trust and their precious life in a scorpion-like person's hands. If you have not already figured it out, people with scorpion-like behaviors seek people with turtle-like behaviors. **People with turtle-like behaviors, beware! Do not make yourself an easy target.**

You may have noticed I did not talk about how people with turtle-like behaviors are born and made. It was not an oversight on my part. I have deliberately chosen not to reveal how people with turtle-like behaviors are born and made. In case my aim for this choice is not apparent to you, I will make it clearer now. I believe there is enough hurt and pain in this world, and I am not interested in helping to create more. I know the power of information and how it helps people get what they want in life.

I have chosen to protect people with turtle-like behaviors all over this globe by not providing any more information about them than is necessary. I decided to do this because I believe people with turtle-like behaviors are now an endangered species, and consistent with this book's purpose, I want to do what I can to help them survive and ultimately thrive!

PART II
Foundational Human Knowledge

To better understand the original scorpion and the turtle fable, we must look more closely at some essential truths concerning foundational human knowledge. By utilizing examples from turtle-like people and scorpion-like people, I will attempt to unpack what and why you need to know all you can.

To accomplish this unpacking, I will refer to what I have learned from many teachers, professors, religious leaders, and ordinary people with great common sense. Also, I will call upon my many years as a behavioral health professional and from my for-profit and not-for-profit leadership experiences. It is a privilege and honor for me to share more of what I have learned from interacting with and helping thousands of clients with turtle-like behaviors and people with scorpion-like behaviors, and from my direct survival experiences from being on this planet for over six decades.

Each story in this book is a mixture of all my experiences put into a story format to assist you in your learning. Therefore, it assures that client-therapist confidentiality is always maintained. That said, I hope you can relate to my stories, but any and all resemblances that may be similar to your life are purely coincidental.

You may want to read through this part of the book to get an overview first, then take each with its story and foundational human knowledge, and spend a week fully digesting it before moving on to Part III. This will allow you an opportunity to cover Part II entirely over thirteen weeks. I have developed a coaching companion workbook and thirteen personal workbooks, journals, and virtual groups to be used with this book to add to your learning experience so you can do life better. Please allow me to encourage you to take advantage of as many of these as you can.

It is an honor and privilege to share some wisdom that I have been given to help you survive our troubling times. I am doing all that I know in the limited time we have together to provide you with the necessary foundational human knowledge and guidance you will need.

As you read each story below, I want you to pick out who is demonstrating scorpion-like and turtle-like behaviors so you can better recognize these behaviors in your own life. You may find there is not always one of them, but there might be two scorpion-like people or two turtle-like people. To give you some additional help to begin with, I will point out to you who is who in the first three stories, then the others will be left for you to find.

CHAPTER FIVE

IS IT JUST SIBLING RIVALRY?

Caught Red-Handed Story

Isabella was the second child in a family of four. She had one younger brother and a younger sister, as well as one older sister named Joan. Her parents were not wealthy and had a modest house. Doctors told their parents, early in their marriage, that they would likely not have children because of something that had to do with their dad. Isabella's older sister Joan was the firstborn and was a pleasant surprise to her parents. Isabella believed they spoiled her older sister Joan because they thought they would never be able to have a child in the first place. When Isabella used the word *spoiled*, she meant whatever her older sister wanted, she always received from her parents, including the best new clothes and shoes.

Isabella and Joan shared a bedroom. Growing up, Isabella often received her older sister's hand-me-down clothes after she was done with them. It would not have been so bad, except the clothes Isabella received were out of style by the time she received them. Her parents bought the rest of her siblings' brand-new garments to wear.

When Isabella was sixteen, she started a part-time job, working after school and on weekends to buy some clothes of her own. She was always very conscious about fashion and searched through many stores, online, and in magazines before deciding what clothes to buy. She liked her job, but she would not have worked if she had not wanted to pick out and buy clothes of her own.

One day after work, Isabella decided to go to a movie theater close by to see a newly released movie. She walked into the movie theater and saw her older sister wearing one of her brand-new outfits that she had never worn. As if this was not enough, her older sister Joan was sitting with the boy Isabella had always had a crush on. Isabella had spoken to her sister so many times about her feelings for this boy.

Isabella acted as though she did not see Joan, quickly walked to a seat, and sat down since the movie was about to start. It was hard for Isabella to concentrate and enjoy the movie because she could not believe her sister would act in such a manner. A single thought kept running through her head: how could Joan take her brand-new designer outfit and go on a date with the same boy she liked and was too shy to express her true feelings to.

Isabella made it through the movie, but as you can imagine, had a hard time focusing on what it was about. When it was over she headed straight home. When she got home Joan was still out as it was getting late, and Isabella was so emotionally exhausted, she fell asleep. She had to get up early to go to work the following day. Isabella got up early the next day, and her sister was still sleeping. Isabella dressed and went off to work, but found herself repeatedly unable to get out of her mind what had happened the previous night.

When she got off work, she went home and confronted her elder sister, asking her whether she had watched any good movies lately. Joan said, "No." Isabella also asked Joan if she had seen a particular outfit of hers that she could not find. Again, her sister replied with a firm "No." At that point, Isabella became so angry she could hardly think straight. She tried hard to keep calm. After taking a few deep breaths, she asked her sister one more question: "Why are you lying to me?"

Her elder sister looked surprised and said, "What are you talking about?"

Isabella replied, "I saw you last night at the movie theater on Main Street wearing my brand-new, never-been-worn designer outfit, and oh, there is more! The worst part was that I saw you on a date with a boy that you know I have a crush on."

Without missing a beat, Isabella's older sister looked her straight in the eye and told her she did not need to wear her ugly outfit, and she could have any boy she chose, and there was nothing she or anybody else could do about it. Isabella dropped her head and she left the room. From that point on, the relationship between Isabella and Joan was never the same. The last I heard, both sisters, to this day, some fifty years later, only talk to each other on major holidays.

Who Is Who?

In this story, Joan has scorpion-like behaviors, and Isabella has turtle-like behaviors.

FOUNDATIONAL HUMAN KNOWLEDGE

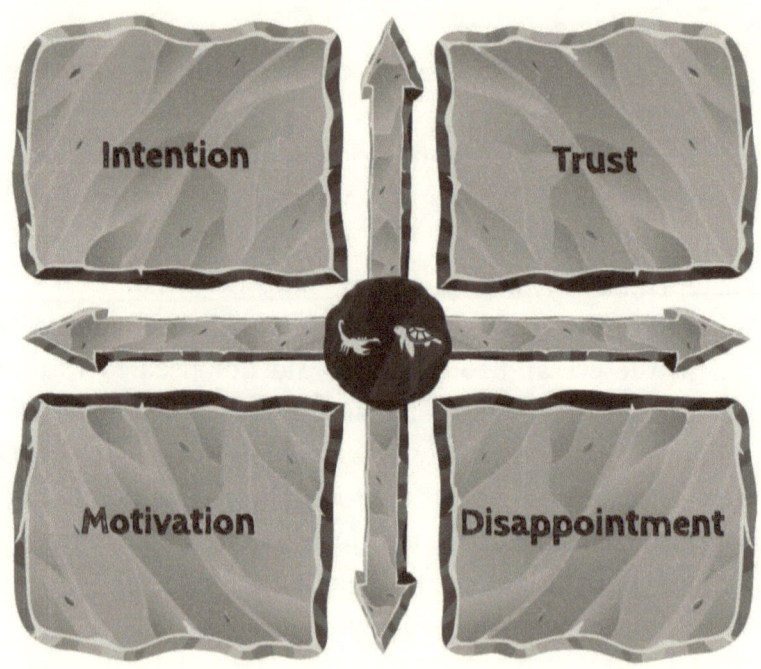

Figure 1: Chapter Five - Foundational Human Knowledge

Intention

> Intention is the why and what that is responsible for and occurs before all human action. It is one's reason for acting.

As human beings, most of us believe we are the highest life forms on the planet. If that is true, then I think one of the things that must separate us from other forms of life is our intention. **Intention involves choice, choice involves options, and options involve some level of free will. I want to go on record by saying, "I believe intention matters."**

To illustrate this further, I would like to share with you something that happened in my own life one fall November evening. How it could have negatively changed my life forever, much more than it did. This November night began like many nights that had preceded it. One unique thing about it was that I had worked particularly late, and I had not had much to eat all day, and I was beginning to get very hungry. Although it was late in the evening, I decided to find a restaurant to eat a late dinner. I found a restaurant still open and had a quick bite.

On my way home, I experienced an unexpected, life-changing event that I remember now some years later as if it happened yesterday. I pulled into a left-turn lane to turn left across a four-lane highway. As I approached it, the arrow turned green for me to make my left turn. I proceeded to the intersection and began my ninety-degree turn. At about a third of the way into the turn, I experienced what I can only describe as a bomb going off in my car. I looked up to the right when I heard the loud impact, and to this day, I am sure I saw a physical shockwave go through the vehicle. Everything went into slow motion until time seemed to catch up with me. My vehicle sustained a strike on the front right side, about two feet from the front of my right front tire. A car traveling about sixty miles an hour had just hit me. My car was spinning in circles until it hit an embankment and slid down a hill to its final stop. I had to use both feet to open my driver's side door and crawl out of my totaled car.

It took me several seconds to realized I had been in a car accident. I found myself in a daze and was in some pain. My anger was beginning to build after I got free from the car. Within a minute or two later, a young man came from the vehicle that had struck me and identified himself as the driver. He called over to me saying, "I am so sorry! I was looking at my GPS, and I did not see the traffic light. I am so sorry." He had blood on his arms and legs. After saying those few words, he simply walked away.

I immediately moved from any anger I had been experiencing to compassion. I thought of my son and my love for him as a parent.

I never saw or talked further to the young man who changed my life that night. I found out later from the police report that he was from out of town and was celebrating his twenty-first birthday.

This accident resulted in over a year of medical treatment for me. Despite the treatments, I still have permanent nerve damage in my body. Although the outcome of this young man's action that night was hurtful and painful on my end, I felt for him and wished him well. I have chosen to accept his heartfelt apology because he did not intend to harm me.

This acceptance allows me to shift my thoughts and feelings of that night to one of compassion toward him. I think it is safe to say I would not have been able to make this shift so quickly or have been so understanding and compassionate toward him if he had intended to harm me. Therefore, for this and other reasons I believe intention matters. I was reminded of something important that night. It is important to look at people's intentions and not only their actions, as this will enable you to act accordingly.

Points and questions you may want to ponder:

Can you find in the story "Caught Red-Handed" where intention plays a role?

Who had what intentions, do you think?

Trust

> Trust is an inherent requirement of human beings to take calculated risks with people. The more one trusts, the more chances one is able and willing to take with others. Fully trusting is the desirable state in which people strive to feel most comfortable with others and their environment.

Trust is necessary to survive and ultimately to thrive in this world. There seems to be two primary ways to look at trust. The first option is to give 100 percent trust to people from the beginning. If they demonstrate they are not trustworthy, then withdraw your trust. The second option is to start with minimal trust and add to it as people show they are trustworthy. Whichever option you choose is your choice, and when you apply it.

I would like to point out that choosing to trust completely leaves you open to being destroyed by others or, at a minimum, being hurt significantly. If you survive being hurt, you will require time and other resources to heal to the point that is possible. I say "possible" because there are things that you or others may not be able to heal from. That said, my experience and education have shown me that much of this world's pain can be either avoided by making good decisions or used by each of us to become even stronger, wiser and more loving human beings.

Yes, I know there is a third option—to shut down, withdraw from society, and become numb. This option makes our hearts harden. The person appears to be alive on the outside, but they are dead on the inside, where no one can see their actual pain. The problem with this choice is that the chooser cannot feel real pain and cannot experience all that is good in life either. Living this way is like taking a trip to the most beautiful place you can imagine on Earth and arriving there wearing eight pairs of heavily tinted sunglasses over your eyes. Subsequently, when someone who knows you just came back asks, "How was your trip, and what did you think of the place you visited?" your only honest response would be, "It was dark!" I hope you can see the many problems with this choice.

Points and questions you may want to ponder:

Can you find in the story "Caught Red-Handed" where trust is involved?

Was there a loss of trust?

Motivation

> Motivation is required for people to act and is like an inner voice saying, "What's in it for me?" The motivation of a person, group, or nation is not constant but changes over time. This is often dependent on both the intention and the situation, including resource availability and timing.

In my thirty-five-year career, I have worked in a leadership role, directly and indirectly in several capacities, with thousands of people. During that time, I learned that there are two primary types of motivation. One is external motivation, which is the motivation originating from outside the person.[13] Sometimes, this type of motivation is not pleasant. If you are like many of us, you have worked mainly for other people and had a boss or supervisor. If you have not yet experienced this, you are likely to do so sometime in your life if you ever work. The times I have spent working for others under their direct supervision have been interesting, to say the least.

Multiple times, I have directly experienced what it is like to work for someone who exemplifies "The Peter Principle," which you may know is a concept in management theory in which people in a hierarchy rise to "their level of incompetence."[14] You can recognize this type of leader because they will try to control you and your work, and they will often take credit for your achievements. They will take advantage of your talents and work ethic. You will never be able to please them because they are so insecure. They rarely praise you unless it gives them an advantage professionally. I can say without any doubt in my mind that this

---

[13] https://www.healthline.com/health/extrinsic-motivation#efficacy.
[14] Peter, L.J., & Hull, R. (1969). The Peter principle.

type of leader only knows how to motivate subordinates through intimidation and fear. They will rarely be interested in whatever is best for you. They only know how to use external motivation to get you to behave and do what they want you to do. For them, it is about power and control through their position. I hope you can tell I am not a fan of this type of ineffective and short-sighted attempt at motivation.

Leadership of others is a high responsibility and can be best accomplished by being a servant leader who leads by example.[15] I have included some of my experiences in this section, primarily, hoping that government leaders, small to medium business owners, and large companies worldwide will re-examine how they choose their leaders and consider redefining their definition of leadership.

Not so long ago, we were reminded, again by another black swan event, just how much we all depend on each other.[16] A worldwide crisis still reminds us that without people such as law enforcement, firefighters, doctors, nurses, therapists, first responders, those in the military, and others all over this world who step up when we are in need, literally risking their lives, many of us would not be here today.

We must learn, acknowledge, and demonstrate by our actions that we finally know and understand human life's actual value! Historically, I have said to anyone who would listen, the greatest resource in this world is the human resource. I ask you, how much more obvious does it need to be?

I am now challenging all leaders across this world to learn how to utilize their leadership role better and demonstrate it by

---

[15] Maxwell, J. C. (1998). The 21 Irrefutable Laws of Leadership: Follow Them and People Will Follow You. Nashville, Tenn.: Thomas Nelson Publishers.
[16] Taleb, N. N. (2007). The Black Swan: The Impact of the Highly Improbable. Random House.

putting their own words into action and effectively employing their influence to improve the human condition. This world will be better for it. This will be a demonstration of true leadership!

The other form of motivation, which I have found is far more powerful and longer-lasting, is called "internal motivation."[17] I believe it is less painful for all involved. This form of motivation is a personal choice that comes from people's own volition. I always prefer internal motivation to external motivation if possible.

Let me provide you with several examples as to how I have come to this conclusion. For instance, internal motivation is essential if you are looking for a close relationship with another person. After all, do you want to be with a person who does not want to be with you? I am sure nobody wants this for themselves because it is exhausting to always do two people's work in keeping the relationship going. I know many of you know what I am talking about here! Another example I can think of involves the difference between working for yourself, being motivated to work long hours to receive all the benefits from your effort, or having to work for someone else for a certain amount of money per hour and trying to decide how much work you are going to do for the little pay you are going to receive.

For many, motivation is about perceived return and value given their effort. No matter what our motivation is, as people, we must have a reason to act. **As human beings, our reasons to act must be meaningful enough for us to exert the energy required.** As we get older and older, this energy becomes more and more limited in supply. So, if you are not only seeking to survive, but thrive, you must look at using your energy very efficiently.

---

[17] Hewett, R. (2023), Dissonance, Reflection and Reframing: Unpacking the Black Box of Motivation Internalization. J. Manage. Stud., 60: 285-312. https://doi.org/10.1111/joms.12878.

Points and questions you may want to ponder:

Can you describe in the story "Caught Red-Handed" where motivation is addressed?

What is its significance?

Disappointment

> **Disappointment is the negative thought and feeling that results when a person gets less than they wanted or expected.**

Initially, disappointment is a state of mind. It begins with a thought. That is good news. Since it starts with a thought, you can avoid much of what would have been a disappointment in your life. Okay, I hope you would like to know how to manage this situation—this avoidance of negative thoughts—better. You can start by choosing to look at life differently from the way you may have in the past. I am not saying it will be easy, but you need to know how to work with this issue as a human being. This is how you do it. Do not count on shortcuts because they will not always be available to fall back on. Sometimes, it takes deliberate action on your part if you want to have the best life possible. This is one such time. If you want to feel less disappointment and the resulting pain, you must examine how you think about things.

Let us examine *disappointment* in context to the story of Isabella and her sister, Joan. I am saying the issue or problem concerns Joan's poor choices, and Joan's choices did not make Isabella a victim. Life can hurt. For many people, it is not about having pain as much as it is about who hurt them. Let me encourage you not to let what happens to you in your life change who you were intended to be. Many in the world say, "Just pick yourself up and get back into the game"! I am saying stop personalizing everything in your life. The world does not revolve around you, no matter what the world tries to make you believe. Please understand, that some things cannot be regarded as true just because the TV, radio, magazines, and the Internet tell you so. It is vital to discover the truth for yourself and not aimlessly take anyone's word for it, not even mine. This is your life, and if you are going to take responsibility for it, you must get involved and learn how to verify for yourself what is real and true!

You might be saying, *This is not fair, Dr. Bill.*

Yes, life sometimes is not fair. That means relationships are sometimes not fair. Parents sometimes are not fair. Bosses sometimes are not fair. Judges are sometimes not fair. Politicians sometimes are not fair. I hope you are getting my point now: people always are not fair. That is just what it is. I am not trying to burst your bubble. I am only trying to help you see the reality of life so you might have fewer feelings of unnecessary disappointment and pain.

If you believe life is fair, you will expect life to be fair, and if you expect life to be fair, you will be disappointed repeatedly. Now that you understand this better, you can avoid many of life's possible disappointments.

Points and questions you may want to ponder:

Can you find in the story "Caught Red-Handed" where disappointment is present and how it could have been minimized?

What is its relevance and to whom?

Life-Changing Learning Opportunities

I want you to consider capturing in writing what comes first into your awareness as you experience each story and the foundational human knowledge I have shared with you. I believe you will gain some additional insights, and it will help you take specific actions in your life, which will help you have the life you have always wanted.

Let me give you an example for illustration and learning purposes only of what I am talking about using this first story. There are no right or wrong answers here. There is just where you are in this moment.

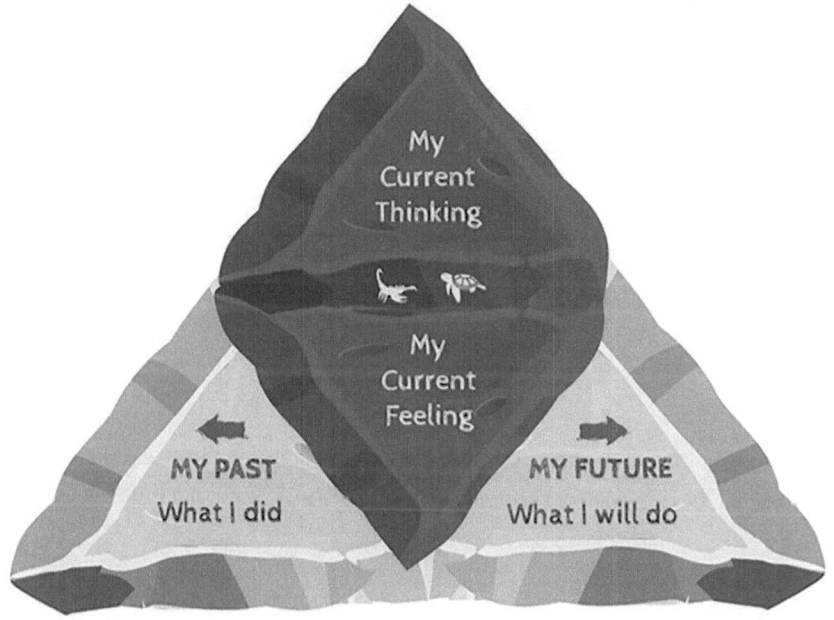

Figure 2: Life-Changing Learning Opportunities Pyramid

My Additional Current Thoughts

Why did Isabella's sister have to be so mean? Look, if that is all that Isabella has to be upset about in her family, she needs to get over it and consider herself lucky. She has a family, a job, and a place to live. Joan was just stupid.

Okay, now I can see that intention matters, but that does not change the fact that people have hurt me. What am I supposed to do with that? Just act like it did not happen?

People always let me down. I do not get my hopes up anymore, especially with guys, because they just play you. I can see now how my expectations affect how I feel. I will not allow other people to control me anymore.

My Current Feelings

I am sad for Isabella. I am angry at her sister. I am confused as to why Isabella did not go to her parents and talk to them about her feelings. I am happy Isabella confronted her sister and did not let her get away with this.

My parents taught us we are to love our family more than anyone else. When I have trusted a family member, I have been hurt very deeply. It seems like they are trying to hurt me more than a regular person I encounter might hurt me. And I do not understand why.

What is trust? I have been hurt like this and much worse, and I do not feel like I can trust people anymore. I feel angry and hurt a lot. I am always upset when people do not respect me. I feel afraid most of the time. I do not feel loved.

Actions That Will Affect My Future

I am going to be more loving to my sister in the future. When I become a mom, I will make sure I talk with my children to find out how they feel about things. I am not going to play favorites with my children.

I will no longer allow myself to get so angry when people do not do what I want. I am going to find a way to heal from the pain I received when I was young. I am going to stop trying to control everyone so I can feel more secure. If people in my current life don't accept me as I am, then I am going to need to find people who do.

I set personal safety boundaries for myself, so anyone who is hurting me now cannot do so in the future. I am going to work on finding ways to forgive people in my life who have hurt me. I know now I must take control of who I allow into my heart.

Now it is your turn:

My Additional Current Thoughts

My Current Feelings

Actions That Will Affect My Future

CHAPTER SIX

LOVE FINDS A WAY

Another Chance Story

Please allow me to share with you a story of a man I will call "Otto". When he was a baby, less than seven months old, his father, Hans, walked away from him.

Otto's father was very well known in his community, a rough man, and somewhat large in stature. He was among the first generation of Americans who grew up in Hungary. He came over with his three brothers to America some twenty years earlier for a better life. Hans had married Sara and they had four children together before their divorce. Hans was at work one day when Sara got her belongings and left their home, never to return. The story told was that she was afraid of Hans because he was a powerful man who had a bad temper and a well-deserved reputation for being a womanizer.

One cold day in February, soon after Sara had left Otto's father, he wrapped up little seven-month-old Otto in a small blanket and took him in a basket to the door of an orphanage. Attached to the blanket was a note that read, *Please take in this boy named Otto and find him a good home.*

Otto spent the next three years as an orphan and he never spoke until one special day. At the orphanage, there were only boys, about fifty in number. They were of different ages, with Otto being the youngest and two seventeen-year-olds being the oldest. No matter how young the orphans were, they had to work to earn their keep. When Otto turned two, he began going with the other boys to tend and milk the cows before breakfast. Throughout the day, he was responsible for other chores.

One day, a woman showed up at the orphanage, looking for a particular child. She even knew the child she was looking for was named Otto. Otto was outside when this woman walked up to him and called him by his name. She said, "Otto, I am here to take you home." At first, Otto did not understand what she meant. For Otto, this was the only home he had ever known. It was early in the morning, and when Otto looked up, the sun was in his eyes, and the woman was surrounded by light all around her. The pretty, well-dressed woman looked like an angel to Otto. She then knelt, looked little Otto in the eyes, and said, "I am your mother, and I have been looking for you for a long time."

Otto could hardly believe what he was hearing and seeing. With tears welling up in his eyes, he said, "Mama, Mama," and jumped into her arms. That was just the beginning of the story for Otto. There is much more to this story, but let us just say for now, Otto's life was never the same again.

Who Is Who?

Otto's father has scorpion-like behaviors, and his mother has turtle-like behaviors in this story.

FOUNDATIONAL HUMAN KNOWLEDGE

Figure 3: Chapter Six - Foundational Human Knowledge

Survival

> **Survival is the built-in need for and the attempt to continue to participate in life for one's own sake and for future generations.**

In school, many of us learned about Darwin's theory.[18] For those who may not recall the details, briefly, it is about how one generation affects the next generation based on the relationship between environment and genetics. As you may recall, environmental experiences that are more useful for survival will influence the current generation's genetics and thus pass on to the next generation, given the individual survives and has offspring. This will continue from one generation to the next, ensuring the survival of the fittest. Individuals without those positive survival characteristics are less likely to survive, given all things being equal. It has been my observation that the need to survive is a part of all creation.

The very point that something exists implies its intention for survival. There are many reasons why something created does not survive. I think it is obvious that there is more going on concerning survival in our so-called civilized societies, than just survival of the fittest. It is well-known that societies worldwide have encouraged and attempted to influence those abilities and characteristics that would enhance and ensure a greater probability of survival of one group or country over another.

I have come to realize, a major problem arises when an individual, group, or government takes the position of survival at all costs. For them, it does not matter what harm is done to others or our planet in their quest to survive.

---

[18] Darwin, C. (1859). The origin of species by means of natural selection (Vol. 247, p. 1859). EA Weeks.

If we are the highest life forms on this planet, then I believe it is up to us all to find a way to survive while creating minimal harm to our environment, other people and all the different forms of life that exist with us.

Points and questions you may want to ponder:

In the story "Another Chance," find where survival is highlighted and describe its role.

Love

> Love is an extremely positive thought, feeling, or action designed to enhance human beings and bring them together to help one another and, in many cases, have children. Love is not just a thought or feeling but is demonstrable.

We were designed to love and to be loved. Can you imagine what it would look like in this world if most humans did not know what it feels like to be genuinely loved? For many people today they do not have to imagine it. They find themselves living in a world that seems not to encourage the love of others and, in many cases, not even love of self. This is a real problem because I have found that a person cannot share love with others when they do not have it within themself.

I once met with a man for several hours who was in his late forties. He spent quite some time sharing his life challenges with me. At some point, I concluded that what he might need to focus on was his close relationships and how he expressed his love to others. I believed these things would help him the most.

A few minutes after telling him this, he looked at me with a look of puzzlement and said, "Dr. Bill, what is love?" He was serious. He did not know what love was. We spent the rest of our time in that session exploring the topic of love.

From that day forward, I realized not everybody knows real love, and I will never again take this for granted. Now I am asking you, "Do you really know what real love is?" If you would like to know, you can find the answer in 1 Corinthians 13:4-8, in a well-known, all-time best-selling book, the Holy Bible.[19]

---

[19] Bible - Windows. (n.d.-b). https://ebible.org/study/?w1=bible&t1=local%3Aeng-web&v1=JN1_1.

A common way people show love is through words and by touch. If you have not noticed, many people say one thing, but do another, especially if they are in scorpion-like mode. Love was never designed to be kept to oneself; it is meant to be shared. I have found that all real love originates from one source and has done so since the beginning of time. If you do not know where love comes from, I hope you will choose to seek the answer until you discover the truth for yourself. It will be a real life changer!

On a personal note, I learned early in life from my mother that "Actions always speak louder than words." She also told me "Sticks and stones may break your bones, but words can never hurt you." I learned that words can hurt very badly. So, I think what she was trying to say to me with love was this: *You have a choice as to how much words will hurt you, but you do not have the same choice with sticks and stones.* I think she was right on both accounts.

Points and questions you may want to ponder:

In the story "Another Chance," how was love demonstrated, and why did it matter?

Fear

> Fear is a natural result of being afraid of something or of thinking that something undesirable might happen. We use it to alert ourselves to a potential threat to our well-being and survival.

I will not ask if you have ever been afraid in your lifetime. That would be an absurd question because we all experience fear shortly after coming into this world and again at times throughout our lives. **With all our exposure to fear, you would think humanity would get used to it by now. To some extent, I believe we have. I do not see how human beings could function daily without learning to manage their fears to a large extent.** There is so much to be potentially afraid of in this world that we will experience fear and sometimes be frightened if we are to survive.

All of us have a built-in will to survive. I use this term in a general sense, which includes courage and all the other attributes a person would need to bring to the table to survive. Human capabilities to manage their fears varies from person to person. A problem can arise when a person experiences too much fear at one time or when its duration is too long. Then, the person's brain can be stuck in fear and might not find a way out on its own.

I grew up enjoying animals of all kinds, and I remember when I was younger seeing a dog chasing its tail until it became exhausted and collapsed. For human beings, fear will literally take the life energy right out of them, much as a dog might chase its tail until it gets exhausted. A lot of people come to see me because of fear. They often present it in different forms, such as poor sleep, anxiety, depression, or obsessive-compulsive disorder (OCD).

The good news is that there are now ways to help people manage fear to a point where they can have a real life and enjoy more of it. It is gratifying for me to see a person frozen by fear return in a short time to fully living. Fear is not meant to be permanent in any way. It helps us to survive threatening situations.

I clearly remember a time in my young childhood, while living in Florida, when we watched the news, and it said there were nuclear missiles in Cuba aimed right at us and ready to launch at any minute. I remember hugging and kissing my mother and her saying goodbye. I was sad, and I thought it would be the last time I would see her again until heaven. She was sitting on an orange couch, smoking a cigarette, while a family friend who had an underground bomb shelter where I would stay led me away. I was five years old at the time.

The nuclear threat to this world is as real now as it has ever been, if not more, but as an adult, I have learned how to manage fear much better. As an adult, I have chosen to put my faith in *love*, not fear.

I get up every day, and I am grateful for the opportunities given me to experience life, no matter how good or hard the day is. I take life the way it is, one second at a time. I would propose you could too. I am not here to tell you that you should not be afraid of anything, because we all know things that can harm us. I am saying that if you want to live your best life, you must find a way to manage fear so that it will not dictate *how* you live your life.

There is a remarkable book that has a lot to say about fear if you would like to know how to conquer your fears. Use any internet browser search of your choice and ask what book has been read the most over the years. There you will find the gift of "Peace beyond all understanding."

Points and questions you may want to ponder:

In the story "Another Chance," where was fear presented, and what effect did it have on each person involved?

Living

> Living meets the minimal requirements to be alive, such as brain function, heartbeat, and other body functions necessary for life. Living is a choice to act and the action one takes to get the most out of being alive by maximizing life opportunities and personal assets.

There are many levels of living. Survival is the first level; the gradation goes all the way to the highest level, which is thriving. I value human life. Since I value human life, I have continued to commit much of my life energy to help others have the best life possible.

Have you ever met or heard of anyone who created himself or herself? When we look at or search for other life forms on Planet Earth or anywhere else, it seems human life is rare. That makes you rare. This is because there is only one you.

Even if you have an identical twin, we all know there is only one unique you. No one has your exact fingerprints. You are a one-of-one! I believe there is something inside you that no other human being has. You are given life not only to live it but to offer your uniqueness to the world. For me, the very fact that you are alive is an indication that you are to live life fully!

So, the question here is, how do you choose to live? I believe the answer to this question will matter not only to you but also to the rest of the world. I can hear some of you saying, "Come on, Dr. Bill, no one cares about how I live my life. What do I have that matters to the world?"

To you, I say, "Yes, they do, and being the real you always matters!"

I know it can be exceedingly difficult because of who you are, living in a world that puts everyone in a box. This box has to do with performance being equal to a person's value. **I believe that since the world did not create us, then the world cannot define our true value.** I believe our true value is given to each of us at birth, and it does not change. We have equal value because we are all human beings.

The greatest differences in the lives of people are what they do with what they have. If you think about it, how each of us lives our lives daily affects many people around us and even our planet. The point I am trying to make is that you are particularly important to the world. How you live your life matters. Please consider living your life in a way that is positive for you and others.

I know it is your life, and it is not my place to tell you how to live it. I always meet and work with those I assist wherever they are in their lives. No matter how good or bad you perceive your life right now, you always have some level of choice, and your choices do matter. Please, consider living life to the fullest by offering others what makes you a one-of-one.

Points and questions you may want to ponder:

Can you find in the story "Another Chance" where living was highlighted and how it changed for all those involved?

Life-Changing Learning Opportunities

Please pause for a moment and list some of your thoughts and feelings from what you have just experienced. After doing this, I recommend you write down the actions you will take to affect your future for the better. Do this based on what comes first to your mind after reading the story with its accompanying foundational human knowledge.

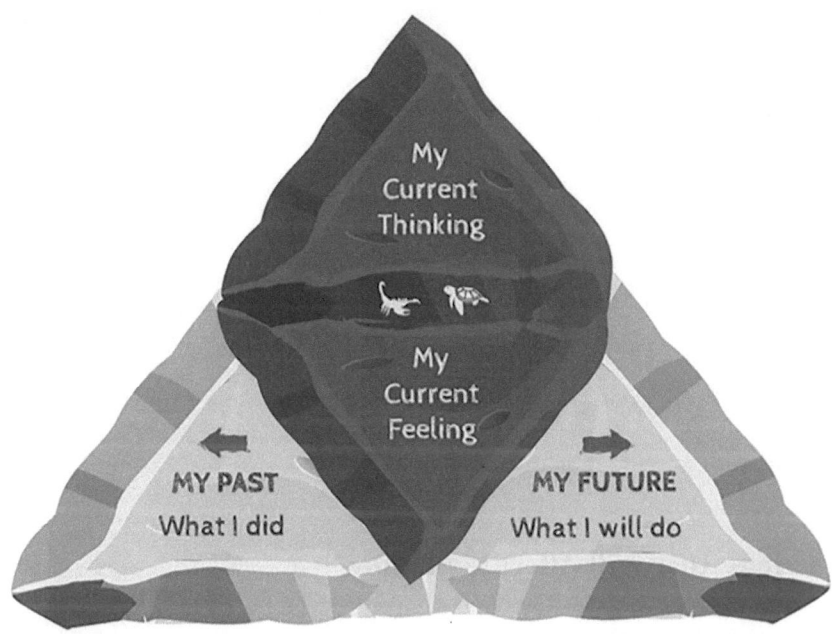

Figure 4: Life-Changing Learning Opportunities Pyramid

My Additional Current Thoughts

My Current Feelings

Actions That Will Affect My Future

CHAPTER SEVEN

ADDICTION AND RELATIONSHIPS DON'T MIX

The Destroyer Story

I received a text from a man named Sam. He wanted to come to visit me to talk about a few things. I responded to him, and we set a date and time for him to come to my office.

When I first met Sam, his body language told me he was sad. There is a lot of literature that looks at how people communicate with one another. Most agree that people only use words to express about 20 to 25 percent of what they want to convey to one another in person. In other words, body language represents about 75 to 80 percent of all communication when one person is with another.[20]

I asked Sam how I might be of assistance to him. Without making any eye contact with me, he said, "It is my wife. I am here because I love my wife!"

---

[20] helpguide.org/articles/relationships-communication/nonverbal-communication.htm.

I asked him to share more about himself and his wife at a level he was comfortable with doing. After wiping his eyes with a tissue, he stated that his beautiful bride was no longer the same. He went on to tell me that he had been married five times and he thought this would be his last wife. He had deliberately chosen her because she was thirty-five years younger than he was. Later, I found out that they had married when he was seventy and she was thirty-five.

He said his current wife took good care of him, including picking out his clothes and making all the travel arrangements for him. They were coming up on their tenth wedding anniversary and had traveled together all over the world as if "joined at the hip." He continued, they always traveled first class, stayed at the best hotels, ate at the finest restaurants, and drank the best wines money could buy.

Then he paused for a moment and said, "To be perfectly honest, we may have done a few drugs along the way and smoked some weed but of course, we never exhaled. I mean, *inhaled*," and then he laughed. He continued, "Now after ten years of blissful marriage, I never thought I would be losing her to liver failure."

His wife had been in the local hospital on and off for the last year. She needed a new liver but could not get on the liver transplant list because she could not stop drinking alcohol. She was too weak to fly to another country, even for experimental treatment, and could hardly walk most of the time. I had several opportunities to meet with Sam over about four months, and I even agreed to meet with him and his wife once at their house. I remember that meeting perfectly. I had never met his wife before, and what stood out to me was her skin color. It was mustard yellow from liver damage. She was dying a slow death.

The three of us talked for several hours about their life, love for one another and her desire for her husband to be strong. Thus, her wish was for him to go on with his life after her passing. Thirty days after I met with this couple at their beautiful home, I received a text from Sam that his wife had passed, and her struggles were now over. He thanked me for all that I had done for the two of them, and I never heard from him again.

Who Is Who?

Sam has scorpion-like behaviors, and his wife has turtle-like behaviors.

FOUNDATIONAL HUMAN KNOWLEDGE

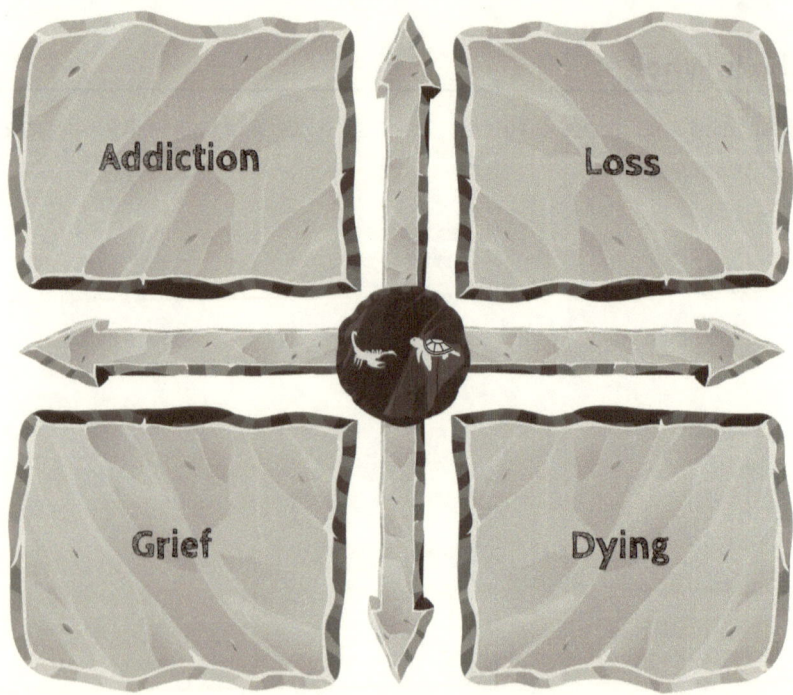

Figure 5: Chapter Seven - Foundational Human Knowledge

Addiction

> **Addiction** is a connection to something or someone you cannot stop voluntarily, no matter the consequences.

Using the definition above, addiction today is common. If you open your eyes and know what to look for, you will see addiction everywhere. Modern human beings are addicted to technology, food, shopping, sex, money, substances, alcohol, status, gambling, power, and control over others, to name a few that are rather obvious.

There are more examples, such as those addicted to pain, counterfeit love, conflict, and hate. If you think about it, I am sure you can come up with a lot more. At this point, I hope you might be tempted to ask, "Why is this the case?" In my many years of life and professional work in the helping profession, I have seen firsthand the inescapable consequences of addictions of all kinds.

If you have had little experience with addiction, consider yourself blessed. However, if you live long enough, you will come face-to-face with it. One of the many characteristics of addiction, is that once formed, it is almost always present in that person and often changes from one substance or form to another.

I vividly remember when I had the unique opportunity to spend four years managing and living at an adult, licensed residential, substance-abuse treatment program in the early 2000s. I provided professional care to over 180 men and women who were in the later stages of their addictions and in a fight for their precious lives. Due to their addictions, most had lost many if not all of their worldly possessions and jobs. They had also lost most of their connection with family and previous friends.

Make no mistake about it; addiction is a destroyer of people. Addiction is no respecter of a person's race, education, social status, wealth, age, gender, country of origin, or anything else. It will not stop on its own until it takes everything of value from its host. As a certified addiction professional (CAP) working in the addiction field, I have found that the best way to manage addiction is not to start one! If addiction has no host, it cannot survive.

Many people who come to see me to improve their lives often discover they are in denial concerning their addictions. It is common after we talk for a while to find out they are addicted to something that does not help them live the life they want. Since many addictions are sanctioned by society, people are easily drawn into them without really understanding the potential consequences.

There are financial gains for many companies to keep people addicted to their products and services. They see it as *just business*; they give you (the customer) what you want, and if they do not do that, someone else will.

You see a few companies raising awareness about how their products or services can be harmful. Many are doing this now because they are legally required to or realize their consumer base is shrinking. They know what I told you earlier that without a host, there can be no addiction. They also know that without addiction, there are less customers, and in the end this is bad for business.

If you are a person who wants to be free from addictions, please consider seeking help from an addiction professional and surround yourself with like-minded people who can provide you with maximum support. Do not try to do it by yourself. I am not saying it cannot be done by yourself; I am just saying, "Why do it all by yourself if you can find support?"

Points and questions you may want to ponder:

Identify addiction's role in Sam's relationship and its effect on his wife in the story "The Destroyer."

Loss

> Loss can come in many forms. It is what one experiences from not winning or from having something that is valued being taken away, and it almost always includes emotional pain.

Even though many people see life as a game, it is clearly not. It is for real! If I were to accept that life was just a game then for many people in this world, it seems there are few winners, and many losers in life. It also seems the winners like it like that and will do all they can to keep it that way.

If you are like most people in this world, you know what loss is because you experience it frequently. Loss is pain. Loss is sadness, and it can take the very life out of you. It is very discouraging to lose repeatedly. I work with people who have had many losses in their lives. They come to me, one by one, sometimes with little hope of their life improving.

One of my greatest joys is when I have the privilege to witness firsthand the human spirit rise up in the middle of great despair and find a deep breath that changes everything! Loss does not have to have the last word. You can triumph over it! From my experience, the biggest challenge with loss is how to get through it so one can get on with living.

I see loss as a valuable part of life; it is expected and is there to help us grow as human beings. When I was a little boy, no one set me aside and told me life would be full of losses. I would not have understood it anyway. Loss is something you must experience yourself to understand fully.

I have had my share of personal and professional losses. Overcoming a loss is a challenging task, and it takes a lot before life becomes colorful again. You must try to hold your ground after a loss. You may be tempted to try to manage it all by yourself. I would ask you to consider reaching out to friends, clergy, family, and, if you have an opportunity, a mental health professional such as a *Scorpions and Turtles Coach*™ when you are ready and able to do so for help.

Loss can be seen as both the end and the beginning, but I would rather see it as the beginning of something different. However, when you are dealing with loss you may not be able to see that it can be the beginning of something much better. Let me give you a few common examples of what I am talking about. What about when a person loses a job and later, finds another that pays even more and comes with a better boss? How about when you are in a relationship and the other person decides to dissolve it, and you find yourself alone. I often hear people say they will just stay alone for the rest of their lives. It is clear to me it is not good to spend most of one's life alone.

I have received texts from former clients who, after some time of healing, have come across the love of their life, and they are sharing a picture of the two of them together with text messages such as, "My life is so much better now, Thank you again, Dr. Bill, for all of your help."

My point here is that sometimes it takes many losses before you can really value and appreciate life fully, better understand what is best for you, and find it. I encourage you never to give up on life, no matter how hard it seems at the time. "This too shall pass." Believe me, I know!

Points and questions you may want to ponder:

What were the losses for Sam and his wife in the story "The Destroyer", and how could they have been avoided?

Grief

> **Grief is a painful human reaction which often accompanies loss. The bigger the loss, the more likely one will experience grief.**

Emotional reactions to grief can include anger, guilt, sadness, anxiety, and despair. Physical reactions of grief can include sleeping problems, appetite changes, and other health challenges, including major illnesses.

Grief comes with being alive. Being alive and grieving is a package deal. It is true that not all human beings share the same experiences of grief in this world. That said, **I do not know of anyone who escapes experiencing grief at some stage in their lives.**

One of the problems we have as humans is that we are not taught about grief; thus, we are not well prepared to manage grief when it comes. Being prepared can mean many things, but it is better to be ready for something than not. I hope you will gain insight into grief from this book and be better able to move through it on your way to living your life to the fullest. Consider this. Less loss equals less grief.

Please allow me to offer you ways to minimize grief and loss. You can do this by being proactive whenever possible. The key is to choose to live your life deliberately and apply what you have learned from the universal foundational human knowledge that I am sharing with you in this book. Due to the way we learn as human beings, I am aware that some people will not fully accept some of what I am sharing. They will need to learn it on their own. I have found that pain can be an amazingly effective teacher.

Many people attempt to deal with grief by trying to escape their negative feelings of loss. Even if you do temporarily find a way, it does not resolve anything. It only compounds the real problems. It is not uncommon for me to see people who have had many losses of varying kinds over their lives, all of which are still unresolved. As most of us do, they have tried many ways to manage their pain and have, to some degree, been successful, but it is still creating problems in their life. They come to me to be free from their past and sometimes their present.

I am known for explaining these things to my clients during my first encounter with them. I know they have come to me with major concerns involving their life, and I know most will leave our time together not being the same. When they leave, I would prefer they not only feel better but also be better than they were when they chose to seek my assistance. Otherwise, what would be the point? I believe in getting to the point right away, so usually, we get directly to work on what is stopping them from living the life they want.

The true answer to what is stopping them most of the time is themselves. Now, that is good news. I have seen so many lives change for the better when people find ways to manage their grief better. Holding on to grief for years will literally shorten your life. If you want absolute freedom, you must confront your losses and your grief!

There are several ways to do this. What seems evident from my years of work as a professional psychotherapist is that many people can find a way to release themselves from years of loss and grief in a relatively short period when they get appropriate help. If you are being held back by loss and grief in your life, let me encourage you to be like many others who have benefited by learning how to release their loss and grief.

I usually get at least one or two texts a week from people who thank me for my help and are so glad they chose to confront their losses. When former clients contact me, my heart is touched in a special way, and it helps keep me motivated to continue to offer my services to those who need them. Please keep those texts and e-mails coming. They really do matter!

Points and questions you may want to ponder:

In what ways do you think grief was part of the couple's story in "The Destroyer"?

Dying

> **Dying is the process of losing a life. It results in no longer having a heartbeat and leads to death.**

The subject of dying is often scary for many people. This fear is often about the unknown. I have met many people who keep wondering what will happen after they breathe out for the last time. Many people do not think about dying as a natural process. The truth is we are not going to live upon this Earth forever. All humans must yield to the normal progression of human life.

Before you get into how dark or how much of a downer this is, I would ask you to look at the glass as half full. Indeed, you do not know how many heartbeats you may have in your lifetime, but you can choose to use every one of them to the maximum degree. I believe death is necessary, and it is an important part of our lives. The knowledge that death is inevitable is there to wake us up! Yes, to wake us up and to alert us to the fact that life is neither guaranteed nor a right. **Life is a gift for human beings to receive openly and use wisely.**

I see people who have a deep feeling of loss over the death of a loved one. It is normal to grieve the loss of someone or something you love. Healthy human beings form attachments as part of living. When something you value greatly is taken from you, it can be as if something dies inside you. Maybe, it does. Hurting is part of life. Did I just say that? I know it is not good to stuff or ignore real pain. It takes a lot of life's energy from you if you choose to hold on to this hurt and not allow this kind of pain to pass.

Many people believe that if they let go of their pain, they must let go of the love they had for what they lost. I do not see it that way. I am here to assure you that your life can be better if you allow yourself to release the pain. Remembering the positives and the love you still have can help you heal and move on to living again! After all, love is what life is about!

It is what helps motivate us to use the time we have wisely. We have a unique and rare opportunity to live life to the fullest! If you are hurting, please allow me to encourage you to let go of the pain, so you can truly live again!

Points and questions you may want to ponder:

How is dying presented in the story, "The Destroyer"?

How did it affect both Sam and his wife?

Life-Changing Learning Opportunities

Please pause for a moment and list some of your thoughts and feelings from what you have just experienced. After doing this, I recommend you write down the actions you will take to affect your future for the better. Do this based on what comes first to your mind after reading the story with its accompanying foundational human knowledge.

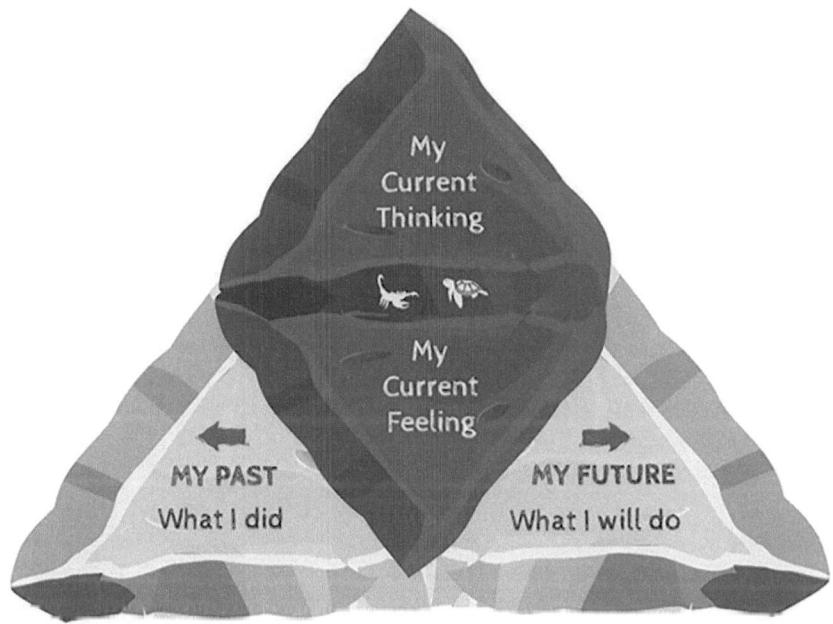

Figure 6: Life-Changing Learning Opportunities Pyramid

My Additional Current Thoughts

My Current Feelings

Actions That Will Affect My Future

CHAPTER EIGHT

IT'S NEVER ENOUGH

What's in It for Me? Story

I recall a session with Tony, a fifty-five-year-old married man, and later with him and his wife. He told me he felt like he had worked in his grandfather's restaurant business as a toddler from the time he could walk. Tony had lost both his parents in an airplane accident when he was just a baby; he was the only survivor. Tony's grandparents had raised him, and his grandfather was the only father he ever knew.

When Tony was seven years old, he discovered that his grandfather, Antonio, had learned to cook when he was a little boy from his mother, Sofia, whom everyone knew all over Italy for her wonderful bread and homemade spaghetti sauce. Sofia made sure her family had the finest meals she could make, and she did all the housework.

Tony's grandfather was extremely hardworking, believing in the philosophy of working hard and playing hard. He drank and smoked cigarettes heavily and was usually out of the house. Tony learned early in life to work hard so he could get whatever he wanted.

He learned not to depend on anybody because no one can be trusted to always be there for you. He would often say he was a self-made man.

At fifty-five, Tony was neither happy nor at peace. He had built a restaurant empire of over three hundred restaurants, had a forty-two-year-old wife, and two children under the age of seven. This was his second marriage.

His first wife of fifteen years had died of lung cancer twelve years earlier. They had no children. I remember Tony's words clearly when he said, "If smoking had not killed her, she would have died eventually from her alcohol consumption, because she drank like a fish."

He then said, "Enough about my first wife," and went on to tell me that what was now causing his unhappiness and taking his peace had to do with his current wife, who was "out of control." That was his perception.

He explained further that his wife, Rachel, was going out all the time with her girlfriends, drinking too much, and coming home late at night. Besides that, he had just bought her a $250,000 red Italian sports car because she "just had to have it." He described himself as a simple man who gets up at 5:30 a.m. and drives a fifteen-year-old pickup truck to work every day. I could see Tony was becoming more and more angry as he was telling me this. I could see the veins sticking out from the sides of his neck, so I suggested he calm down for the benefit of his health and take a short water break.

Upon returning, we resumed our conversation. He said it was Rachel, his wife, who told him to see me because she had tried to tell him that she was unhappy, and he just did not seem to get it. She thought that if he talked to someone who was a professional, it might help. She wanted him to come first, and then she wanted them both to meet with me. Some time passed after I had met with Tony before receiving a request from his wife for the three of us to meet.

The moment we met, it was clear to me that Tony and Rachel had their own way of communicating with each other. I mean there was a lot of sarcasm from each of them toward one another, and then they would look at each other and laugh. Rachel said Tony was acting like an old man because he never wanted to go out anymore and was very controlling. I asked her to explain a little more. She gave me several examples, after which Tony could hardly keep seated. It was clear from his body language that he did not appreciate or agree with what she was saying about him. When she had finished, Tony spoke up and said his wife was acting as if she was still single, drank too much, and was sending out sexual messages to every man in the room when she went out at night. She said, "I do not know why he is complaining. I give him sex once a week. Just look at the old man. I do not think he could handle more than that. It might finish him off." A few minutes later, the session was over, and they walked out and thanked me.

Who is who?

Who had scorpion-like behaviors? _____

Who had turtle-like behaviors? _____

FOUNDATIONAL HUMAN KNOWLEDGE

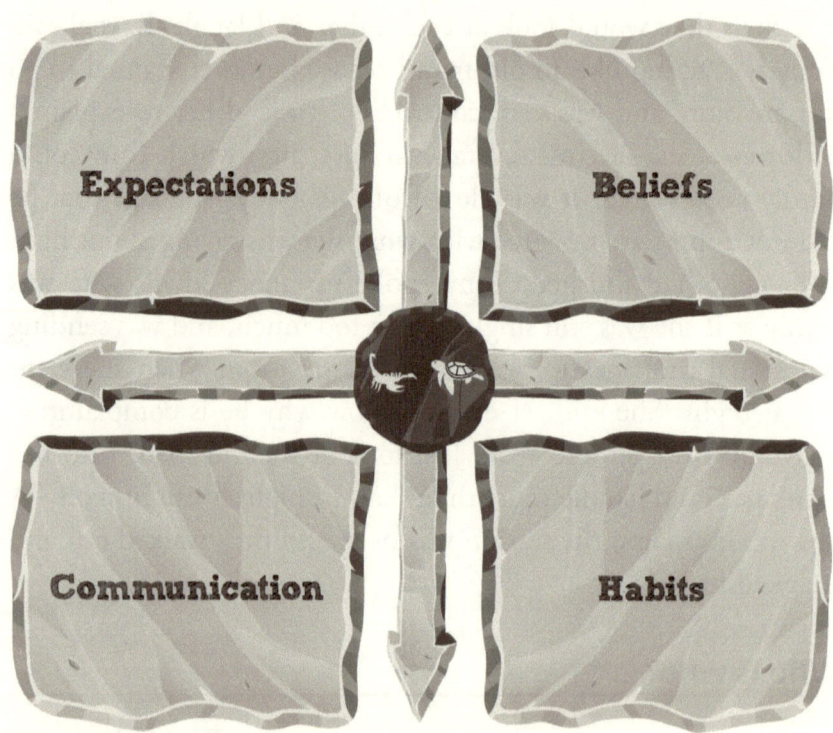

Figure 7: Chapter Eight - Foundational Human Knowledge

Expectations

> Expectations are the specific thoughts one has about how life should be. It is that which helps us know more, because we seek greater understanding.

How we interpret our life lies within each of us. Most human beings have the power and authority to determine their expectations and adjust them as required. I like that. That means you can live your life in true freedom, no matter your circumstances. Did you get that? One of the keys to this involves being aware of your expectations and choosing what you will do with them, particularly if they are not met.

As a young child, I was told many of my expectations were unrealistic. I was not only told but was punished for having expectations that did not match my circumstances perfectly. At the time, I had no idea where my expectations came from; I just knew I had them. I believed in them so strongly even punishment was unable to change them. At that time, holding on to my expectations and beliefs depicted me as a problem child to some people. I have always known my circumstances were not who I am. If I could stay on course, one day my circumstances would change and be in better alignment with my beliefs and expectations.

As a result, I suffered very much. Yes, you will pay a price for holding on to your beliefs and expectations when others who are in power around you disagree with you. I am not recommending anyone do what I did as a child. I have become much wiser over the years and have learned to pick my battles very carefully. I have learned it is common to lose battles before you can win the war. Winning the war means always finding ways to have the best life you can, no matter your circumstances during your brief stay on this planet. Adjusting your expectations is a requirement for most of us. It can make a real difference if one wants to experience life in a balanced way.

I said *balanced* because I know living can be difficult, but it does not have to take all the peace, joy, and happiness from you. Your feelings belong to you, remember? You are the only one who can make you feel. Stand up to this world and do not let it make you something you are not. Let the world know you are here and your life matters. Let what *love* and good which is inside you triumph. You are the light and the salt of the world.[21] Be who you really are!

Let us come together and expect this world will turn around and begin to focus on what is right and good in people. Let us encourage each other as opposed to focusing on what is wrong or bad. Let each of us rise to the occasion contributing to this world in a way that leaves it better than we found it. Some might say, "I have high expectations concerning what positive and good human beings are capable of." They would be right. I will make no apology for my beliefs and expectations toward humankind.

Points and questions you may want to ponder:

In the story "What's in it for Me?" what were the expectations of Rachel and Tony, and do you think their expectations were met?

---

[21] https://ebible.org/study/?w1=bible&t1=local%3Aeng-web&v1=MT5_13.

Beliefs

> Beliefs are core thoughts people have concerning truth that drives their behavior.

The power of belief cannot be overstated. The belief in something is inherent in all human beings. In life, another great challenge we have is what to believe and what not to believe. There is so much information available today on any topic or subject you can imagine. Often, there are multiple viewpoints that are in direct conflict with one another.

Being human comes with challenges such as not having all the answers to all of life's questions. We just currently do not know many things, and we may never know all of them. It is virtually impossible to survive as a human being without believing in something or someone. I have experienced this in my practice as well as in my own personal life. There is something that is foundational and absolutely critical to living an exceptional life. It is now my pleasure to share it with you. It is the importance of believing in that which is greater than yourself. I am not saying you can sit back and expect life to take care of itself. What I am saying is there is more to life than just you. None of us is the center of the universe. **Your beliefs act as a foundation for the rest of your life.**

We form our core beliefs mostly in our early years.[22] Though difficult to change I have discovered it is possible to do so. It is also possible to believe strongly in someone or something and yet be very wrong. Your belief or lack of belief can change your reality, but it can never change truth. As you may have

---

[22] https://connect.springerpub.com/content/sgrjcp/32/1/67.

noticed in this book, I am using the words *Truth* and truth in two different ways. *Truth* is another name for God, and truth denotes that something is true or factual.

I am not telling you what to believe in; that is something you must discover for yourself. However, I have found that if you let Truth be your guide, you will find greater understanding. You can then use this to form beliefs that will be more helpful to you in living your best life.

Points and questions you may want to ponder:

Describe who had what beliefs in the story "What's in it for Me?".

How do you think the beliefs of the couple affected each of them in their lives?

Communication

> Communication is the method people use to express themselves to others; it most often involves writing, speaking, touch, and using body language.

One of the things that separate human beings from other life forms is communication. I think most people think of their fellow humans as primarily communicating with words verbally and in writing. It is true we humans do a lot of talking and writing. Have you ever noticed that some people may not use many words at all, and most people repeatedly use the same words? When it comes to using words, what I have found in my practice, it does matter what you say. That said, the problem is often not *what* you say, but *how you say what you say*. As we grow up and receive a formal education, we learn how to use written language more.

Let us look at another way human beings communicate with one another. Most human beings have the option of using touch as a means of communication, either positively or negatively. It is vital in our lives when we are young to learn how to communicate using words and touch.

I saved the third way humans primarily communicate until last. It only happens when two people can see each other while communicating, and is not limited to being next to one another. This form of communication is body language. You already know how important this form of communication is. Usually, couples, family, friends, and other professionals get incredibly good at reading people's body language. That said, most people are not aware of the messages they send to each other through their body language. In my profession, I have discovered that no matter which of the ways you choose to communicate, communication can still be misunderstood.

A great deal of my work revolves around how to help people improve their communication with others. The major challenge that

I have experienced in working with people is that they are unaware of their responsibility concerning communication. Many people believe they have the right to express themselves in any way they please.

I want to raise an important point around communication that I regularly bring up when working with people. Communication is not just one person expressing himself or herself. Yes, communication is about conveying something to another, but it can be much more than that. Communication that matters is about being heard, understood, and often being cared about; in other words, it is about being effective. Thus, effective communication is about you and the delivery of what you want to convey to the audience. If you are going to be more effective in the way you communicate, you must present in a way others can understand.

You now understand you have the initial responsibility as the sender of the information to help the receiver "get it clearly." Blaming others for being misunderstood is no longer necessary. I know it is frustrating at times, but try writing a book. I believe it is worth the effort to communicate effectively.

Points and questions you may want to ponder:

In the story "What's in It for Me?," what are the different types of communication that were used by the two members of the coupleship?

How do you think the couple could have improved their communication with one another?

Habits

> Habits are repetitive thoughts, feelings, and behaviors that become internalized and automatic.

Your brain controls habits. You learned a few things about your brain earlier in this book. You may know, your brain is designed to pursue pleasure and avoid pain. You may not realize it, but the human brain uses chemicals, such as the neurotransmitter dopamine, to reinforce the experience of pleasure in our bodies. Over time, this dopamine release will create habits in the form of behaviors on our part.[23] Habits may be either seen as good or bad by you or others depending on the circumstances. You might be aware of some of your habits, and at the same time, you may have other habits you are unaware of until being told about them by another person.

The more certain habits are reinforced, the stronger they get and the harder they are to change. I will take a wild guess and say you probably know how challenging it can be to break some habits. Am I right?

Some years ago, I came face-to-face with a habit I had developed quite early in my life. I was a serious coffee drinker. I could barely get out of bed without drinking at least two cups of coffee. I continued to drink coffee all through the day. After looking at the role and importance of coffee in my life, I decided to break this long-standing habit of over fifty years. I have nothing against coffee; to this day, I like coffee even though I have not had a drop for over fifteen years. I am sure you might be wondering, "How

---
[23] Ambrosi, P., & Lerner, T. N. (2022). Striatonigrostriatal circuit architecture for disinhibition of dopamine signaling. Cell Reports, 40(7), 111228.

was he able to pull that off?" I realized I had been using coffee in unhealthy ways, and I needed to make a change. I am so glad I did.

I have found other ways to get myself up in the morning and through the day. I have also saved money, which I have chosen to use in better ways. I did what I did, not because it was easy or that someone else made me stop. I did it because it was the right thing for me to do. That does not mean I will not one day choose to drink coffee again, it means it will be my choice not based on a habit. With all habits or anything else in life, I believe it is up to each person to make what they believe to be the best decisions for their own lives while considering others' wishes.

I am happy to now provide you with how to break bad habits if you decide to break a habit or two. Please allow me to offer you a few tips that I have learned along the way. First, you can use your knowledge of your brain to help you break a bad habit. You will need to make use of a part of your brain known as the prefrontal cortex. Because you know your brain seeks pleasure when it can, you can seek its help to do this. Think of something else and find creative ways to reward yourself with something good for you before and while taking deliberate action to discontinue or break a bad habit. By doing this, your brain will begin to focus, rewire, and disconnect itself from your bad habit. Over time, it will get easier and easier to let go of bad habits so you can embrace your better, new habits. This adaptive process of your brain is known as neuroplasticity.[24]

Another tip is to get an accountability partner like a *Scorpions and Turtles' Coach*™ who can be there to encourage you to stay on your chosen course. Also, you want to tell as many people as you can who are important to you that you are going to break

---

[24] Sweatt, J.D. (2016), Neural plasticity and behavior – sixty years of conceptual advances. J. Neurochem., 139: 179-199. https://doi.org/10.1111/jnc.13580.

such a habit. "Why would you want to do this?" I have come to understand that until you share what you are doing with people who matter in your life, you are not really "all in."

Remember, we may not do the things we want to do, but we often do what we must. Besides, people who care about you are there to help you.

Points and questions you may want to ponder:

What habits do you think affected the couple's relationship in the story, "What's in it for Me?"

Do you think these habits were helpful?

Life-Changing Learning Opportunities

Please pause for a moment and list some of your thoughts and feelings from what you have just experienced. After doing this, I recommend you write down the actions you will take to affect your future for the better. Do this based on what comes first to your mind after reading the story with its accompanying foundational human knowledge.

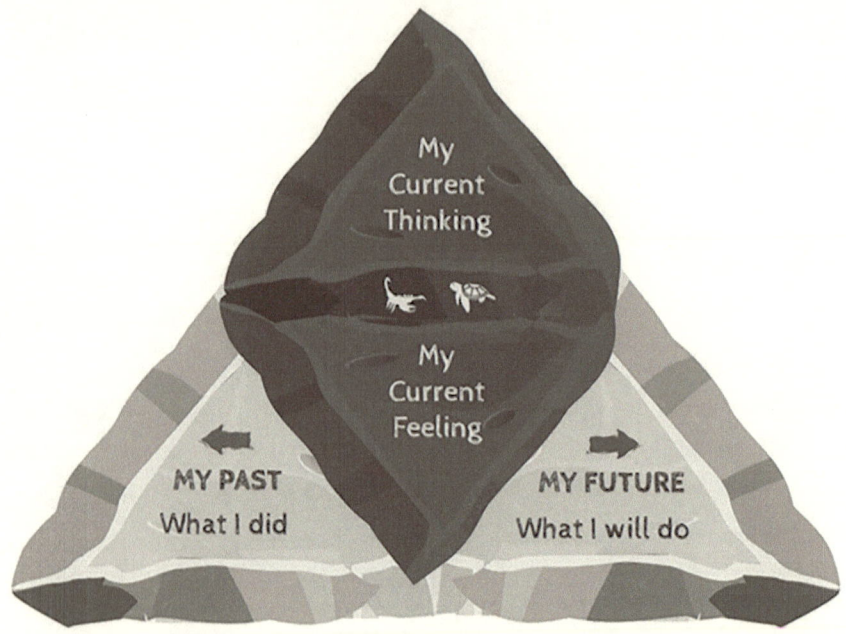

Figure 8: Life-Changing Learning Opportunities Pyramid

My Additional Current Thoughts

My Current Feelings

Actions That Will Affect My Future

CHAPTER NINE

WHAT ABOUT ME?

Exhausted Story

Emma, the wife of a cardiologist, came to see me a few years back. She was in her mid-forties with four children. She had met her husband in high school and married him shortly after he finished his residency program. Emma was dressed casually. She looked and acted very tired.

We spent some time in small talk during the first part of our meeting. Small talk is used when you first meet someone, and you want to feel him or her out to see if you can trust them before you share anything that might be important to you or sensitive in nature.

After about thirty minutes, Emma said, "Dr. Bill, I am here because I am exhausted and I do not think I can do this wife thing anymore. My husband and children are taking all the life out of me." She explained that her husband gets up early every day and has his morning meal waiting for him when he gets up. She goes back to bed for about an hour and a half until her four children get up, and she then feeds them. After they eat, she takes them to school. Two of them go to the same public school, and the other two go to the same private school.

Usually, on the way home from dropping them off at their schools, she stops long enough to get a cup of coffee at a drive through. Once home, she also has three dogs and two cats to take care of as well. One of her dogs is quite old and must have his food made especially for him. She makes it herself, combining different meats and vitamins, which she puts in the blender to make it soft for her sweet old dog to eat. Before she goes to pick up her children from school, there is also house cleaning, which takes several hours. Once she picks up her children from school, she often takes them to after-school activities such as ballet and karate classes. All her children are involved in soccer so that is how most weekends are spent.

Her husband is always working and when he is not, he is sleeping. Emma is left to take care of all these things without him. This has been going on day after day, for the last fifteen years. I wrapped up the last few moments of our time together, talking with her about what she does for herself. It was a challenge for her to think of anything.

Who is who?

Who had scorpion-like behaviors? _____

Who had turtle-like behaviors? _____

FOUNDATIONAL HUMAN KNOWLEDGE

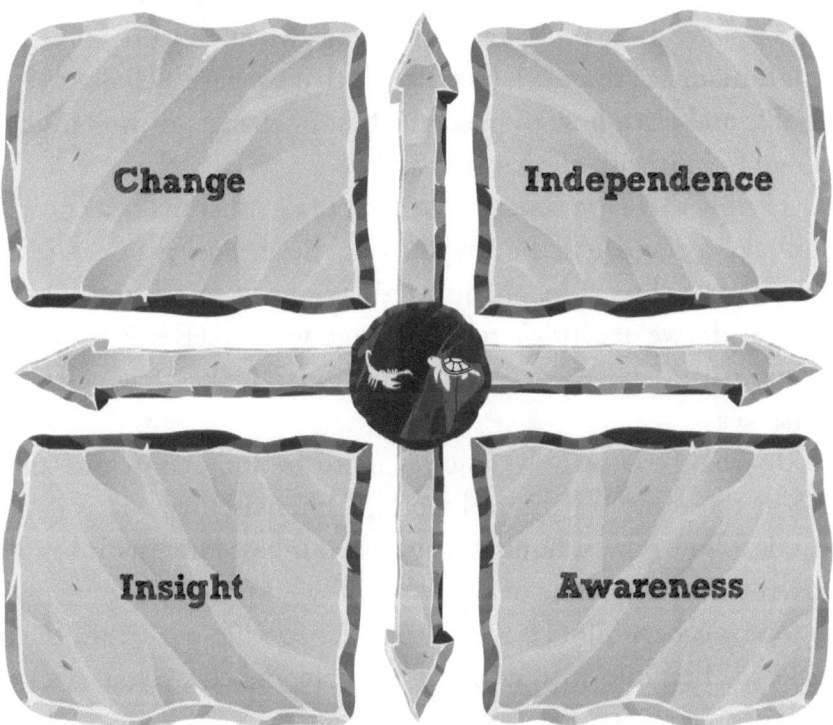

Figure 9: Chapter Nine - Foundational Human Knowledge

Change

> Change is to modify or make different.

To change or not to change? Do you really think you have a choice? You do have the ability to choose to some degree. People seem to have more problems with change when they do not want it or initiate it. I think what matters is that we have a choice to be flexible and learn how to make the best of change, or we can dig in and fight it with all that we have!

I know there are times when each of us must make a choice and take a stand based on what we believe. Positive change is helpful and should be encouraged. We need to ask ourselves: "When do we accept or reject change we perceive as positive or negative?" I believe each of us must make that call for ourselves.

To change effectively requires us to be fully conscious and live in the reality of the real world. Otherwise, we will just be lost or follow others, hoping they have our best interests at heart. Given the current state of the world, I would not advise anyone to follow others blindly. Please consider seeking out truth, then make the best informed decisions you can and check your reality with people you trust.

I implore you, do not give up your right to think for yourself. This is one of those rights worth holding on to tightly. If you do not choose to use it, history has proven you will likely lose it! If you need to change, do it because it is best for you and those you love. Do it because it is the right thing to do!

Points and questions you may want to ponder:

Was change a problem for anyone in the story "Exhausted"?

What changes if any do you think might be helpful and for whom?

Do you think Emma could continue to live as she did?

Independence

> Independence is the ability to choose for oneself, as demonstrated by selecting and acting on options, without being forced.

I have spoken to many scientists who believe there is no such thing as independence. I am not here to debate the matter. I know that throughout time, across this world, human beings fight and die for their independence and yours, even to this day. If it does not exist, then so many have given so much in vain! **I believe each of us is unique and similar by being dependent and independent at the same time.** This is one of the greatest mysteries of the universe and creation. How can we live on this planet and not lose ourselves? For many, the answer is, they cannot. It seems to me that it is a worthwhile ambition to pursue independence in the context of the realities of dependence. Due to the enormous amount of sacrifice rendered by others, we each have the opportunity for a measure of independence. I see so many people who have given up on being who they could be. They just quit.

I am not able to judge another, nor would I if I were. I can only advocate for the survival of hope. Hope in the future of humankind. If there is no independence, then the present must be like the past, and the future must be like the present. I do not buy it, and I hope you do not either.

I have found that responsibility that comes with independence. Without responsibility, independence can be potentially life threatening. All the parents out there know children often want independence as soon as they can get it. In North America and in some other parts of the world children may want to drive a car, stay out all night, or not go to school. They want to have the independence to do what they want.

As a result, I see children who are treated and given independence as if they were adults. I do not believe we do a service to our children or society when we provide them with everything they want at any given time, to keep them calm. I see children learning and growing into adulthood who believe they are entitled to everything because the world revolves around them. It should be no surprise that the world's children are the future, and we as responsible adults will harvest what we plant and thus reap what we sow.

Points and questions you may want to ponder:

Do you think Emma in the story "Exhausted" was independent?

Consider how this affected her life.

Insight

> Insight is a state of mind that results in a more accurate understanding of what is. Insight is that which helps us know more because we seek greater understanding.

One of the most rewarding parts of my job is bring innovation to the counseling field by utilizing talk therapy and neurofeedback.[25] I work with people helping them find effective ways to increase their insight and to find creative solutions to their challenges so they can do life better. Insight for me is a result of tuning in as opposed to tuning out. Try talking with people who often only come to see you because they believe they do not have any other options, and at the same time, they really do not want to be there. I see this mostly when I work with couples. One person may be there to try to find ways to improve and continue the relationship, while the other may not seem as interested.

Hence, many people's challenges with insight are due to being in a crisis and in a self-protection mode all the time. I have noticed that it is less likely one will have the best life possible if one has little insight into one's life. Yes, better insight helps you to choose the life you want more effectively, and it helps you along the way to get there. Without good insight, you might as well be a leaf floating in the wind, going wherever the wind takes you with no ability to direct yourself. By the way, insight is what you are receiving right now. Congratulations!

If you think about it, you are well on your way to living a better life. Hold on, do not stop now. There is more! To acquire insight, you are likely to hear and be in situations you would

---

[25] Ninaus, M., Kober, S. E., Witte, M. H., Koschutnig, K., Neuper, C., & Wood, G. (2015). Brain volumetry and self-regulation of brain activity relevant for neurofeedback. Biological Psychology, 110, 126–133. https://doi.org/10.1016/j.biopsycho.2015.07.009.

rather avoid because they may involve discomfort. **If you have learned to avoid pain at all costs, you cannot gain maximum insight.** You must resist going to your "happy place" or retreating into your virtual imaginary world. I usually find that insight requires me to seek it out deliberately. You must be present in the moment, no matter how uncomfortable you may be. The good news is that as you practice this, you will get better at it.

I promise you the worst part is at the beginning, breaking old habits and starting to create new ones. From what you have recently chosen to learn, I know you are on the right track to doing just that.

Points and questions you may want to ponder:

Do you think Emma in the story "Exhausted", gained any insight into her life?

Do you think she will do anything with her insight to improve her life and the life of her family?

Awareness

> Awareness is knowing what is happening.

Awareness can be a matter of life and death. Have you ever been somewhere where it just did not feel right? Maybe the hairs on the back of your head stood up. That is awareness. Your design as a human being includes the ability to be aware. The problem with awareness is that we can never have enough. I hear people say they do not understand why they did not see something before it got worse. They often get down on themselves when they finally become aware. I do my best to help them understand it takes what it takes before becoming more aware.

Nobody is always fully aware of all things. If you are hard on yourself for not seeing something coming, please give yourself a break. In the scorpion and the turtle fable, the turtle had some awareness, as most of us do, but something overrode it. That is why we can be aware, to some extent, but still find ourselves moving forward and ending up being stung.

I know, it has happened to me. Has it ever happened to you? If you are completely honest with yourself, your answer is likely to be, "Yes, Dr. Bill, more than once." Okay, it happens to all of us.

You might be asking, "How can being stung happen less, or perhaps how can it be avoided?" Those are legitimate questions. To begin with, I know it is difficult to be aware if one is not living in the moment. Many people are moving so fast in life they are not able to see what is right in front of them.

Let me provide you with just one example from my own life. I am *into* sports cars, and I may have a heavy accelerator foot from time to time. I can be cruising along at a good pace, and then it is as though someone poured ice water on me, surprising me. I look down, see the speedometer, and I say to myself, "I did not realize I was going that fast," so I slow down. This used to happen more when I was on the phone or thinking of work while driving. I was not fully present in those moments. I think this sometimes happened because I have driven so many miles over my lifetime. I have now learned that I must guard against going into autopilot. I do not own a self-driving car yet; I am still responsible for driving safely.

I think going into autopilot is like sleepwalking in many ways. Sometimes, people come to my office and appear to have been on autopilot or sleepwalking for decades. Their awareness of what is happening around them is exceptionally low, and that is the first area where I begin to help them.

It is essential to have good awareness. Otherwise, you will not be able to make the best decisions in your life. If one makes poor decisions, then one's life is so much less than it could be. It is never too late to improve your awareness by staying in the present.

Additionally, you need to be careful of your emotional reactions regarding what you are aware of too. **Your emotions can override your thinking. You must not forget this important truth.** Being in the moment and monitoring your emotions will help you become more aware of what is going on in your life.

It also helps if you take care of your brain by not abusing alcohol, nicotine, and other drugs. I know that is understood, but I am the writer of this book, so I invoked the writer's privilege on this one. It is that important. If you are involved in these abusive things, let me encourage you to do whatever it takes including contacting a *Scorpions and Turtles' Coach*™ so you can release them from your life. Remember, there is only one you!

Points and questions you may want to ponder:

How much awareness did Emma in the story "Exhausted" have as to why she could not go on in her marriage?

Do you think that if she had greater awareness, it might have helped her decide to leave her marriage or stay?

Life-Changing Learning Opportunities

Please pause for a moment and list some of your thoughts and feelings from what you have just experienced. After doing this, I recommend you write down the actions you will take to affect your future for the better. Do this based on what comes first to your mind after reading the story with its accompanying foundational human knowledge.

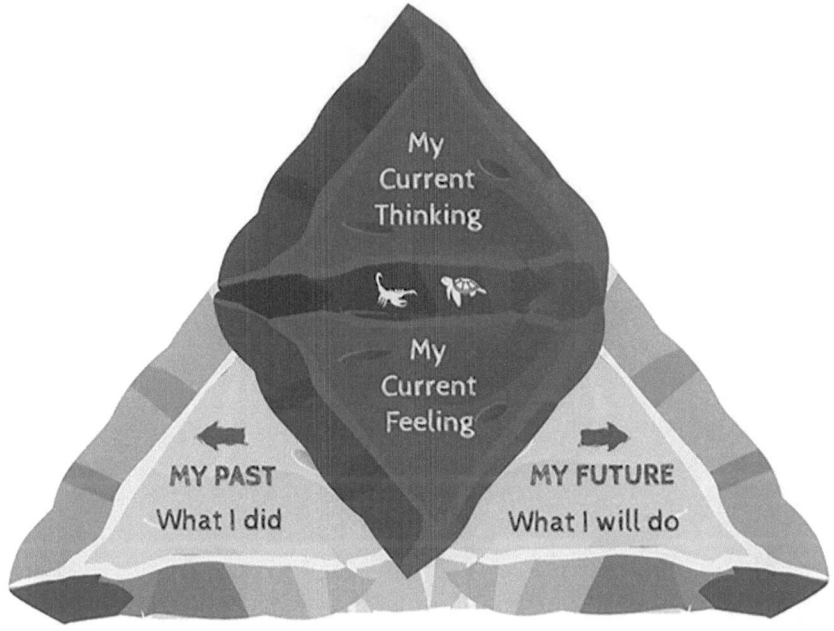

Figure 10: Life-Changing Learning Opportunities Pyramid

My Additional Current Thoughts

My Current Feelings

Actions That Will Affect My Future

CHAPTER TEN

GOOD DECISION OR NOT?

Choices Story

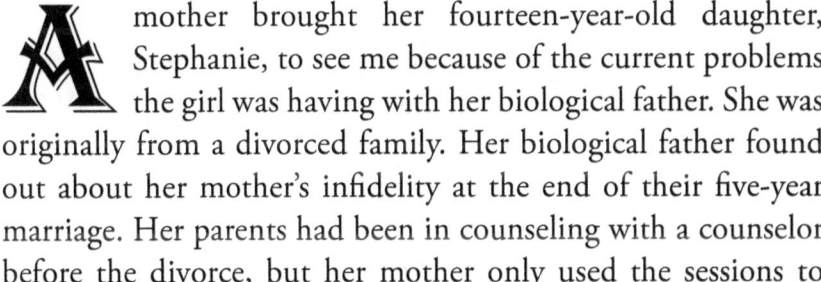mother brought her fourteen-year-old daughter, Stephanie, to see me because of the current problems the girl was having with her biological father. She was originally from a divorced family. Her biological father found out about her mother's infidelity at the end of their five-year marriage. Her parents had been in counseling with a counselor before the divorce, but her mother only used the sessions to complain about the father.

Stephanie's biological father, whom I met several times, provided me with this information. The girl had asked her mother about her biological father and was told he had anger problems. Her mother was concerned about the girl growing up in such an environment, which is why her mother filed for divorce from her father just after Stephanie's first birthday. In the first four years of the girl's life, her mother had three husbands, and the mother and child lived in five houses.

The divorce bankrupted her biological father. The judge decided he had to pay for his ex-wife's bills and to pay for child support, medical, life insurance, and a college fund for Stephanie. Her father worked two jobs, almost twenty hours a day, seven days a week, just to cover everything.

One day at the age of ten, during a visitation weekend that just happened to be on Father's Day, Stephanie told her father that she had chosen to be full-time with her mother and new husband. This was because they had more money, a better house for her, and a new infinity SUV. During the eleven years after the divorce, Stephanie's mother had been a stay-at-home parent. Now married to her fifth husband, she indicated she had no interest in ever working outside the home. She claimed she was entitled to her current husband's money, which his mother recently had left him after she passed on—millions of dollars.

Stephanie was angry at her biological father, saying she hates him and wishes he were dead. She says her mother has ADHD, is not very smart, nor very pretty. From watching her mother, Stephanie says she has learned that manipulation works well.

Before Stephanie became of legal age, I saw her three or four times in my office. I did not see her more because her mother decided Stephanie did not need counseling any longer.

Stephanie's father never had another conversation with his daughter after she turned ten because, through legal maneuvering, he was not allowed to see her until she turned eighteen years old. I am aware her father has reached out to her over two hundred times by text with no reply, using the phone number provided for her by his ex-wife.

I recently received an email from the father stating his daughter is now twenty-seven-years old and has never reached out to him.

He said he prays every night for his prodigal daughter and believes his only child will return to him one day.

I replied to his email and encouraged him to keep the faith!

Who is who?

Who had scorpion-like behaviors? _____

Who had turtle-like behaviors? _____

FOUNDATIONAL HUMAN KNOWLEDGE

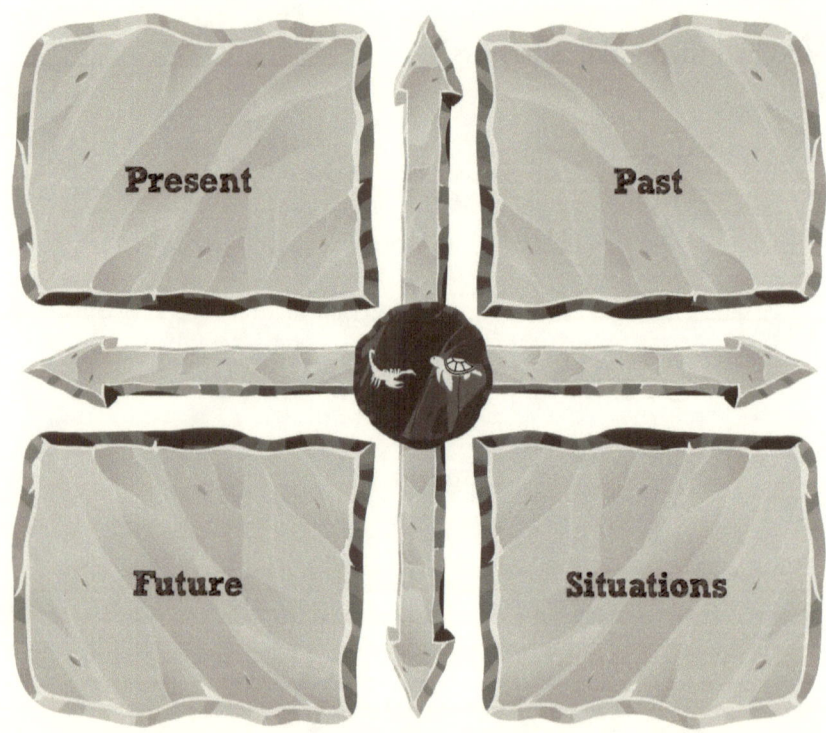

Figure 11: Chapter Ten - Foundational Human Knowledge

Present

> Present is the current part of time, which is now.

How much time do you spend immersed in the present? There is a fine line between thinking about doing something and doing it in the present moment. Technically, the present is the shortest part of time from which we can benefit. Because we live in such a fast-paced world that is more and more difficult to navigate, most of humanity has little time to ponder their lives, even on a good day. We are too busy in the present being reactive to our environment. It is as if we are caught in a big storm, and it is all hands on deck.

The present is where all the action dwells. It makes the doing part of our lives possible. This part of time provides a very brief and important moment and opportunity to experience being in the now. The present is where changes you make can affect your future for better or worse.

It helps to be as prepared as you can be for what life holds for you. How you do this is by learning from your past and focusing your attention on the now. You will have less pain if you choose to prepare instead of just reacting to what life hands you.

I find many people are not living in the present but are living in either the past or the future; still others are in escape mode all the time. This is a rough way to live and is rarely satisfying. I compare this type of living to having one leg on one side of a barbed-wire fence and the other leg on the other side. It is not the ideal place to be if you do not have to be, for all the obvious reasons.

If you are not benefiting from the present as much as you want, I would ask you to consider what I am offering you in this unique self-improvement book. Consider making deliberate positive changes right now in your life to the degree that it is possible.

Points and questions you may want to ponder:

Was the girl's father in the story "Choices" living in the present?

How do you think his daughter's decision to act as if her father did not matter or exist affected her?

Past

> Past is the part of time that has already occurred.

The past is an integral part of time. We are designed to remember the past so we can benefit from what worked best and not keep repeating the same mistakes to have the best life possible.

That is a wild thought if you think about it! It is as if the past is not the past anymore. It seems our thoughts can move in and out of time without limitations or restrictions. This ability to use the past for learning is just one of the things that makes us extraordinary.

Because we can think not only in the present but also about the past and the possible future, there is a real danger that comes with this ability to manipulate time in our minds. The danger is how it can affect our emotions in the present and thus our future. I have spoken to many people who have found themselves in real pain because they brought their past to the present. I have seen many problems created by people who habitually do this, whether intentionally or not.

The main challenge becomes this: What does one do if one's past is not all positive? When I say *do*, I mean do now because technically, the past does not exist anymore; that is why it is called the past. We know human beings can bring the past into the present due to having memory, and our thoughts about the past affect both the present and the future. This is often the case when the present has negative characteristics like our past.

Due to our need for survival, our brains default to a position of reminding us of past negative experiences that are possible in the present. Our brain may think, "Been there. Done that! Not again!" or "Here we go again!" The good news is that you can do something to alter this automatic or habitual process.

I am here to keep you from being a prisoner of your negative past. The secret is to monitor your thoughts by being fully awake and alert while screening your thoughts for relevancy in your present.

Points and questions you may want to ponder:

Was the girl's father in the story "Choices" living in the past?

Was the father's daughter living in the past?

Future

> Future is the time yet to happen. The future is an unknown part of time, and it has no guarantees.

I believe the future was originally designed and given to us as I stated earlier to improve our lives and the lives of others by providing us the opportunity to learn from the past and do something different in the present.

As I get older, one striking thing about the future becomes more apparent. It is just how fast the present becomes the past, which makes the future less and less. We only have so many heartbeats in our lifetime because we are human beings. One of the real ironies of life is that by the time we realize the number, it is too late, our present is gone, and there is no tomorrow.

Due to the possibility of a future, a real seduction comes with it. People worldwide think they have lots of time and opportunity for a better life. As you know, life takes so much more than just possibility. Do you know anybody who does not want a better future? You, maybe? I did not think so!

Nonetheless, there are real problems that can come from the future, too. I have learned that the future is not always positive and can even be hurtful as I perceive it. I also know most people insist on spending a lot of their present moments thinking about what future they want to have and even more, time trying to find ways to get there. I understand the benefits of examining the now and planning for one's future as much as is healthy. **It's important to find a balance in planning for the future while living in the present.** You can do both by immersing yourself in the now and allowing yourself to fully enjoy life as it is. By doing this, you may discover that you are more than okay, and your life is not as bad as it seems, at least for now!

It appears not everyone agrees with me. I realize many people want more and more; they believe there is never enough of what they want. This belief puts them in a constant state of dissatisfaction. This dissatisfaction drives each of them as if caught up in an outer space gravitational field, the event horizon of a "black hole." They are being drawn closer and closer to its center until they are never seen or heard from again.[26]

Have you noticed this world is constantly pushing all of us with targeted messages through various media forms to compare ourselves with others? We are told to compare what we have with what we think is possible and then spend our now time and money to get more in the future. A future with more becomes the primary goal. The world says there is always the need for more and more!

I have seen how destructive this can be to people of all ages. Many people are often dissatisfied with their lives because they compare their lives to those of others. Therefore, I have decided to share this important truth with you: you are a one-of-one and can only seek to be the best you can possibly be.

I am now going to talk directly to those who are intentionally keeping people down and in bondage by encouraging them to be in a state of constant dissatisfaction. I will try to be as clear as possible. Your day has come. You are no longer free to benefit directly and live your dreams while others suffer. I say to you, "Let the people go!"

It is time for us all to open our eyes and embrace the real world. We can no longer afford to be driven by the illusion of "more is better," and make that mantra be our absolute goal for

---

[26] Brito, R., Buonanno, A., & Raymond, V. (2018). Black-hole spectroscopy by making full use of gravitational-wave modeling. Physical Review D, 98(8), 084038.

the future. What happened to "satisfaction"? What happened to "enough is enough"? What happened to "I am good"? I am glad you asked. I believe what has happened over the years is that many people have become accustomed to having more and more of what they want with less and less effort. They no longer think or care about *need* and are left with "I want!" They do not believe they can live without what they now want.

In my practice, I rarely hear "I need," anymore. It has been replaced by "I want" by children and adults. I know *want* and *need* can be the same, but they do not have to be. I will return to this later in this book when I talk about our human footprint. You may be thinking, "What? Dr. Bill, I have been digging your book up to this point. Why did you have to go and ruin it with so much truth." Let me explain. It is written, "The truth will set you free."[27] I want you to be completely free! Free from sleepwalking through life. Free to make the future the best it can be and to enjoy all the blessings that are yours to receive. It is now time to wake up! If not now, when? In the future?

Points and questions you may want to ponder:

Do you think the father's thoughts concerning the future with his daughter in the story "Choices" will help or hurt him to have the best life possible?

---

[27] https://ebible.org/study/?w1=bible&t1=local%3Aeng-web&v1=JN8_32.

Situations

> Situations are the context within which we exist and experience life as human beings. They occur throughout our lifetime.

You may be aware that situations are not always entirely under your control. Did I just say that? That was not easy to say, and I have discovered it is even harder for most of us to accept. If it is easy for you, then you are the exception. In my private practice, it is relatively common for me to hear a person saying, "It seemed like the thing to do at the time, Dr. Bill."

Over the years, I have come to understand what people are trying to tell me. They are saying that after they evaluated their current situation and made deliberate decisions, they took action that may or may not have been the best for them and the people they cared for so much.

In case you have not noticed or remembered, human beings are reactive to their environments. This is important to the overall survival of our species. That said, the problem arises when we react too quickly or do not fully understand the situation. When this happens, it can lead to unanticipated challenges and difficulties in our lives. To those who have such challenges, I recommend they practice giving themselves more time before they act. You might be asking, "What does that look like?" It can be as simple as counting silently to yourself, saying, *one thousand one and one thousand two, and one thousand three*, all the way up to *one thousand six*, while at the same time being aware of your breathing. It is important to take deep breaths and breathe more slowly when you are facing a difficult situation. This is because your brain needs as much oxygen as it can get when under stress.

It boils down to the better you take care of your brain, the better your brain will take care of you! The better your brain takes care of you, the better life you will have. It is that simple.

Points and questions you may want to ponder:

What situation did the father find himself in with his daughter in the story "Choices"?

Could he have done anything different that would have helped his daughter realize how much he loved her?

How do you think the situation the daughter found herself in affected her decision to choose her mother over her father instead of being able to be with both?

Life-Changing Learning Opportunities

Please pause for a moment and list some of your thoughts and feelings from what you have just experienced. After doing this, I recommend you write down the actions you will take to affect your future for the better. Do this based on what comes first to your mind after reading the story with its accompanying foundational human knowledge.

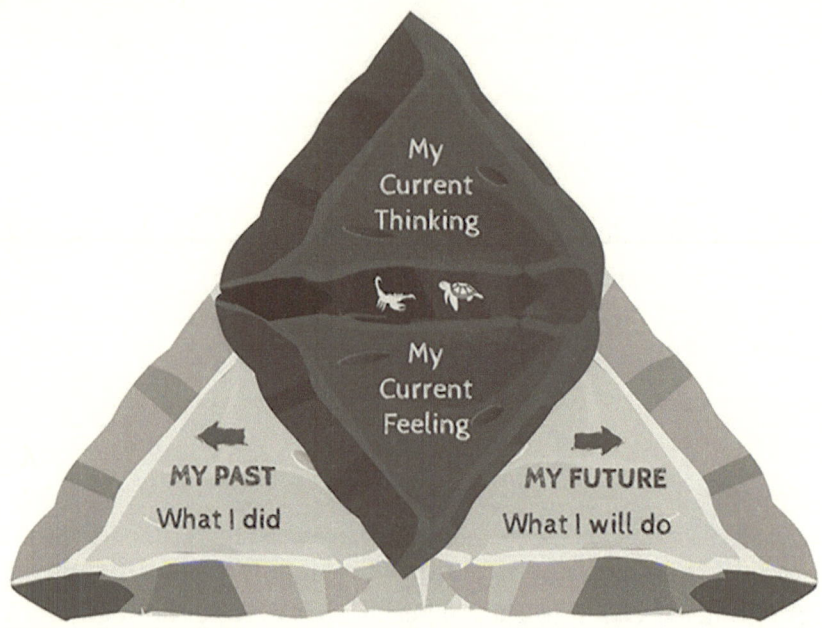

Figure 12: Life-Changing Learning Opportunities Pyramid

My Additional Current Thoughts

My Current Feelings

Actions That Will Affect My Future

CHAPTER ELEVEN

IT'S A SECRET

Ulterior Motives Story

It is common for me to receive a text from someone who lives in another country who would like me to assist them. I see people in my office, provide phone sessions and video sessions over secure internet connections in which I offer counseling and life coaching all over the world. In the instance I recall here, I received a text from a man living in another country. He was planning to come over to the United States for business reasons in several weeks and wanted to come to my office to spend three hours in a session with me. His main desire was to discuss some relationship challenges he was having with his wife at that time.

For me, time can seem to go by very fast and several weeks can seem like several days. Before I knew it, this man (I will refer to him as Bob) knocked on my door. I opened the door, and Bob said, "I am here to see Dr. Bill."

I replied, "You have found him."

We shook hands and moved further into my office to sit in some comfortable chairs, so we could proceed with our time together. Bob appeared to be excited to see me. He said he wanted to talk to someone for some time now, about what had been happening in his marriage. He had never been comfortable doing so until now.

He went on to say he was born in North Carolina, joined the air force after he graduated from college at twenty-three, and shipped overseas, where he had been stationed for the last four years. This was where he had met his wife. After drinking some water from the table next to him, he went on to tell me he had been happy in his marriage in the beginning, but to be perfectly honest, he had been unhappy for a long time before deciding to reach out for help.

He looked at me and said, "My wife has this thing about the clothes I wear. She is always telling me not to wear certain types of clothes because she says they look cheap, and she is embarrassed to be out with me in public for fear someone might see us. Every other time I try to get dressed, she wants to pick out everything I wear. I tell her I am not a child, and she will not give up unless I let her do what she wants. That bothers me sometimes. I can deal with that, but what really bothers me is what happened this year.

"My wife was born in the country of my current military job assignment. I am a nuclear engineer. I have spent most of my life learning in school and never thought I would get married so soon. I mean, I am only twenty-seven. I know a lot about engineering, but I must admit, I do not understand much about women, and I do not understand my wife at all! I give her everything. She has a great house, a car, beautiful clothes, whatever she wants, and yet all she does is complain. When we are with other people, she acts as if she is so happy and as though we have a close and caring relationship, but when we are alone, she is just the opposite. Nothing is good enough.

"Dr. Bill, I am so tired of it. I do not even like going home anymore. I find all kinds of reasons to be out of the house and away from her. This is what I have been doing for many months.

"About four months ago, while I was out one night, one of my co-workers said to me, "Is it okay if I ask you a question?" After a long day's work, I had just finished my first tall one to calm my nerves from a stressful day. I said, "Of course!" He asked me what college I had attended and went on to inquire if they had taught me how to speak the language of the country where we were. I was surprised a bit by his question; it seemed to hit me unexpectedly. I had been in that country for four years. He and I had been co-workers that whole time, and he had never asked me this before.

"I took another drink and said, 'I went to school in North Carolina in the States, but I did not learn this language there. My wife taught me how to speak over the last three years.' He seemed to take a long, hard look at me, and then he smiled. I said, 'What?' and was becoming a little annoyed.

"He said, 'Can I be honest with you? I mean, we are not just co-workers but friends, right?' I assured him we were and again asked him to tell me what was on his mind. There was no preparation whatsoever for what he was going to say to me. He asked me if I had noticed that when I spoke the local language to girls, they often giggled and laughed.

"I said, 'Sometimes.' He said, 'And men, do they look at you somewhat funny?' I said, 'Sometimes, so what is your point? I know I am still learning the language.' He then stated, 'Well, the truth is you are not speaking it correctly. Your speech sounds like that of a little girl.' I said, 'What?' He said, 'You do not talk like an adult.' I said, 'You must be drunk!' He said, 'I am just telling you the truth, Man!' We finished a few more beers, and I went home.

"It took me a couple of days to think about what my friend told me before I decided to confront my wife, who as I said, was my language teacher. I will never forget what it was like. I sat across from her and told her I had some strange reactions from people when I spoke the language, she had been teaching me, and one of my co-workers finally told me why. I asked her why she had taught me to speak the language that way.

"She replied, 'Yes, I am so smart, I taught you the language that way so that when other women hear you speak, they would not be attracted to you because you talk, Hee-hee, like an immature girl.' Her eyes gleamed with delight."

We talked some more until our time was up and he said he felt much better, thanked me for my time and help, and left my office.

Who is who?

Who had scorpion-like behaviors? _____

Who had turtle-like behaviors?_____

FOUNDATIONAL HUMAN KNOWLEDGE

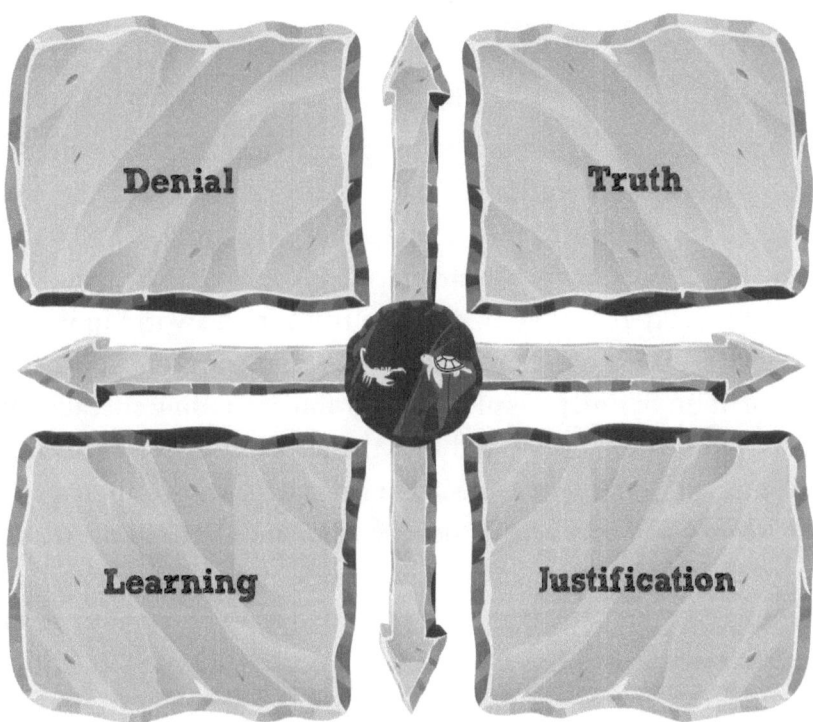

Figure 13: Chapter Eleven - Foundational Human Knowledge

Denial

> Denial may be the most common mental state human beings' function in when they are in survival mode. Denial is designed to buy time for a person to process the truth that can be overwhelming in the moment while they try to manage in a complex world.

To be "in denial" is to be fooling yourself about the reality of your situation. As a human being, I have come to realize that it is almost impossible not to be in denial at least some of the time. Have you ever met people who are in denial about being in denial? I meet them every week in my private practice. My reason for saying this is that it is often hard to discern the truth in the world in which we live. I find it extremely difficult to find a trusted source of information in order to gain a greater understanding. Because of this, I do my homework and find the facts out myself if I can. I recommend you do the same if you believe the truth still matters.

Regularly, I meet with people who have given up on the truth and have become blind followers doing what the pack says they should do. Denial from a psychological point of view can be necessary. It can be helpful when we face extreme difficulties in our lives that we cannot deal with immediately.[28] Since our brain needs to survive, and so does the rest of us, sometimes we automatically default and deny the significance of a threat that is causing us to be afraid or overwhelmed.

This can happen in cases such as the sudden loss of a loved one or other severe trauma. It gives us time to sort through the truth without it destroying us. Okay, I hope you now better understand

---

[28] https://www.psychologytoday.com/us/basics/defense-mechanisms.

how denial plays an essential role in our lives. At this point, you might be saying, "Is there more to denial than the positives." Yes, sometimes being in denial is not positive. Denial is no longer beneficial to us if it lasts too long, or we use it throughout our lifetime to avoid general life events.

This happens when someone overuses denial from childhood to adulthood. This overuse can contribute to a person not developing emotionally at the same rate as their chronological age. I have worked with people who were fifty years old chronologically. However, emotionally their age was closer to sixteen or even younger— an adult on the outside, but still a child on the inside.

I see this a lot when people come to me with magical thinking or live in a made-up world, and they are no longer children but adults. **There are times when denial is your friend, but this friendship is not meant to last forever.**

There is a time when none of us can keep running from *Truth* any longer. The day we stop running is the day we begin to understand ourselves better and move toward fulfilling our destinies.

Points and questions you may want to ponder:

What role did denial play in the story "Ulterior Motives," and who was in denial about what?

Truth

> Truth is that for which we seek, which does not change based on opinion, and is real in this world.

When it comes to being a person, my definition of truth is being authentic and honest based on who you were designed to be.

I believe we live in a predominantly unreal world. Early in our lives, we receive a considerable amount of training on behaving in this unreal world. This training is called socialization. The socialization process includes education, which has a specific purpose. The more socialized we are, the more unreal we may become. Many people have become more and more at odds with their very design. **Over time some people have become speakers of words without meaning.** No wonder more and more people have stopped either listening or believing in anything.

Humankind most assuredly has lost its way. I believe there is still hope for all of us here on Earth. This hope resides in *Truth*. Some people describe Truth as a small voice that they hear in their heads or a gut feeling they feel from time to time, telling them that they are not living their best life. When one is living a dishonest life, it is a form of bondage. I want to encourage you to seek *Truth* throughout your life if you want to reach your true potential.

Points and questions you may want to ponder:

What was real and unreal about the couple and their relationship in the story "Ulterior Motives"?

Learning

> **Learning is obtaining skills and knowledge by personal experience through one's study and from others' teachings.**

Are you aware that there are two primary ways to learn? One way is to learn from others. I believe you can always learn from others if you take the time to pay close attention and open your mind. Everyone you meet has something to teach you about the world and yourself. From others, you can learn what to do and what not to do.

Many people do not like the second way of learning, from our experience. I have found that learning from others is often quicker and can involve a whole lot less pain than learning everything from your own life experiences, sometimes known as "the school of hard knocks." That said, the main advantage of learning from your own direct experience is that if you are like most of us, you are likely to remember your own experiences better than learning from others.

When we each came into this world, we knew nothing as newborns. For most of us, our lives started with significant confusion and chaos. What a way to start, huh? That is how it is, whether we like it or not; we do not have a vote on the matter. The first thing we learn is how to survive from one moment to the next. Many across this globe may never go any further because that is a full-time job. But for others, they could go on, yet choose not to for reasons only known to them.

I believe our lives are not our own. What you do or do not choose to do with your life affects others. Your choice to thrive could help many people worldwide survive, and others even thrive. For these reasons and many more, I would propose once that you learn to survive, you do not stop there but go on to ultimately learn how to thrive. I hope and pray that this book will assist you in doing this.

On a personal note, I recall a Thanksgiving dinner I attended in my then eighty-five-year-old mother's home. I was enjoying this wonderful meal when my mother said, "Dr. Bill, will you ever get out of school?" Momma liked calling me Dr. Bill. I found that out some years earlier.

I said, "Mama, people come to me for help in their lives from all over the world, and I cannot share what I do not have with them. I cannot promise you that I will not pursue a seventh college degree or stop learning. I do not have that luxury!"

To this, she replied, "How do you like the salad?"

It is vital to your future that you never stop learning! From your very first breath to your last, I hope you can see just how dependent your life is on learning. We are more likely to thank people from whom we learn what to do, but when did you last thank someone for teaching you something you should not do? Which is more important? I will leave that to you to think about!

Points and questions you may want to ponder:

What did you learn in the story "Ulterior Motives" about relationships?

What would you have done if you were the husband in this story?

Would you have stayed in the relationship?

Justification

> Justification is a commonly used reason people create and accept to explain their actions being right or just.

Being a human being involves being a life form that has a brain and a body. It is not your hands and feet that make life decisions. It is your brain. Have you ever heard others say the only reason we have a body is for the brain to survive? We use our brains to reason. Therefore, our thoughts come first before all actions, which, of course, originate from our brain.

Part of how we reason involves finding justification for our thoughts, feelings, and actions in our daily life. I share all of this with you to help you better understand, how a human being uses an acceptable reason for their thoughts, feelings, and actions to believe they are justified. This belief of being justified can conflict with society and is how change occurs throughout the world. **It is important to note that one can feel justified in one's actions and still be so wrong in one's conclusions and judgment.**

I am not trying to say that some actions are not instinctual, because I believe many are. For example, the blinking of one's eye when something is approaching is the brain's means of protecting the eye, and it happens without any conscious awareness or direction by the individual. Due to our instincts, we can sometimes use justification without really thinking it through. This is but one of the many challenges we must face over our lifetime.

I have found most people prefer to be right. So often, there is more to life than just being justifiably correct. What ties all this together is the need to survive. Survival is everything to a human being, and it is always primary. You may be saying to yourself, what about those situations when people choose to give their lives for others? My response is that it is about survival, anyway you look at it, even when a person decides to give up their survival for the survival of others.

Points and questions you may want to ponder:

How was justification used in the story "Ulterior Motives" and by whom?

Have you ever used justification to take action?

Life-Changing Learning Opportunities

Please pause for a moment and list some of your thoughts and feelings from what you have just experienced. After doing this, I recommend you write down the actions you will take to affect your future for the better. Do this based on what comes first to your mind after reading the story with its accompanying foundational human knowledge.

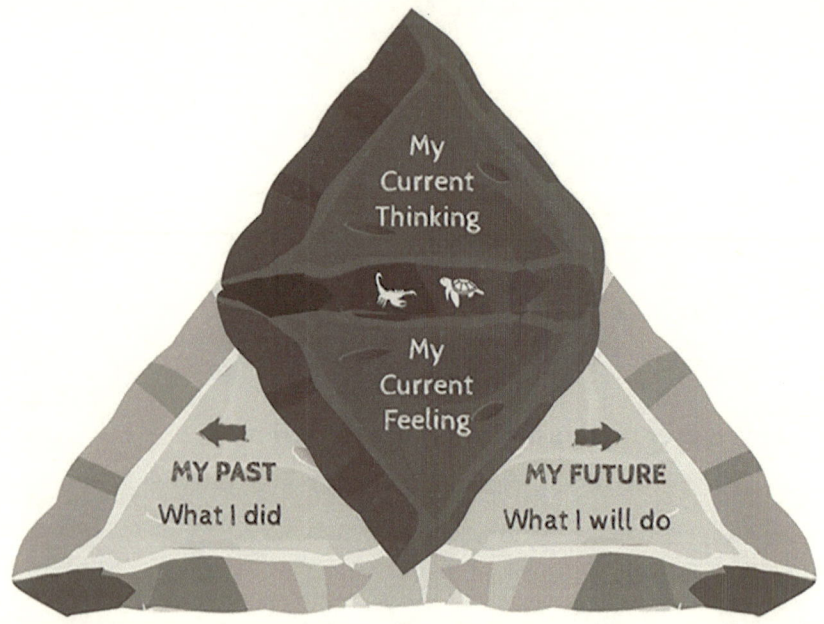

Figure 14: Life-Changing Learning Opportunities Pyramid

My Additional Current Thoughts

My Current Feelings

Actions That Will Affect My Future

CHAPTER TWELVE

IT'S ALL ABOUT THE MONEY

What Friendship? Story

Wanda told me what happened to her after she rented office space from a so-called friend and fellow professional who owned an office suite and needed another tenant. My colleague had known her fellow professional for many years. She had been a shoulder to lean on and someone to talk to when Wanda was going through a long and difficult divorce. My colleague thought she had a true friend she could trust with the most private things that concerned her life.

What follows are more details. One day, they were talking, and the fellow professional said she had a room she would only rent to the right person and asked if my colleague would be interested.

Wanda looked at it and agreed to sign a two-year lease for the office space. It seemed like a great fit. After all, she was going to be leasing from a friend. They had discussed her needs and agreed to refer clients to one another when appropriate. As part of that agreement, my colleague's new landlord promised that she would not bring in someone in the same line of work as my friend.

Wanda had been leasing office space for about a year when she decided it was time to take a vacation. So she did. When she returned to work, she noticed a new tenant had moved into an available space in the same offices, just two doors down from hers. She asked the receptionist, whom she knew well, who had moved in and what their line of work was. Wanda was told it was a business offering the same services as her own, and the receptionist could no longer refer clients to Wanda, as she must now refer them to the new office renter. It seemed Wanda's landlord had formed an informal partnership with the new tenant and was getting a kickback.

A week went by before my colleague had an opportunity to confront her old friend and landlord about this new development and the violation of their oral agreement. When Wanda confronted her landlord, she received a blank stare and was told, "It is just business!"

My colleague told me she could hardly believe her ears. She felt hurt because she thought they had a friendship and wondered how money could be more important than friendship. It seemed it was for her landlord. Wanda had another eleven months on her lease, and her instincts told her to leave right away. But instead, she waited until the end of her lease, thereby meeting her commitment. She then found another office space and moved out.

For the last eleven months my colleague has had a different relationship with her landlord. She said she could hardly wait to get away from those offices.

Some years later, after she had moved out and no longer talked with or leased from this so-called friend, Wanda saw pictures of her ex-husband and her former landlord together on a social media site. They were apparently on a date. My colleague was just heartbroken and felt betrayed beyond measure.

Over time, we talked more about it together, and she healed. As part of her healing, I am pleased to say that she bought her own office to work in and is now quite happy.

Who is who?

Who had scorpion-like behaviors? _____

Who had turtle-like behaviors? _____

FOUNDATIONAL HUMAN KNOWLEDGE

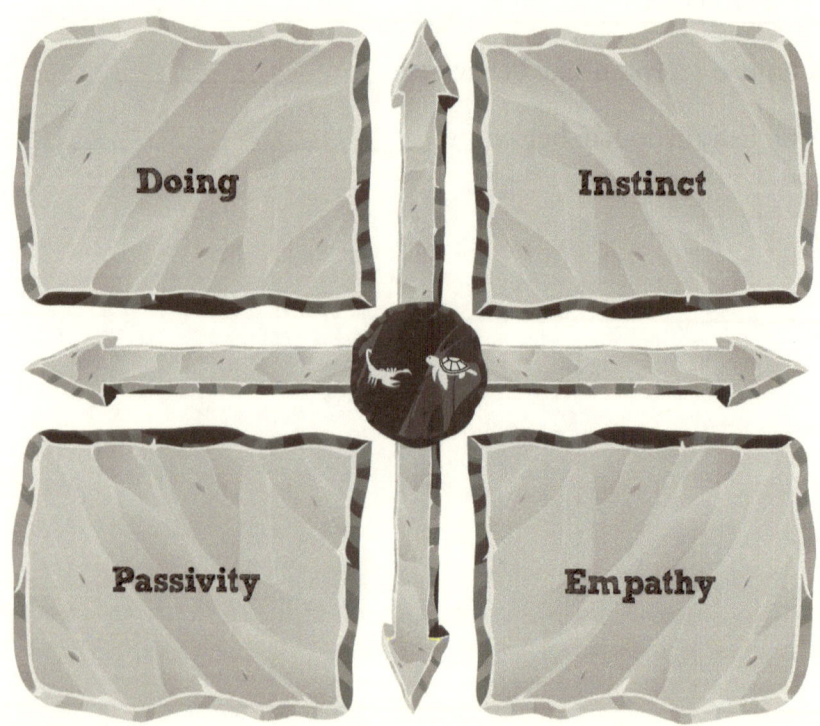

Figure 15: Chapter Twelve - Foundational Human Knowledge

Doing

> **Doing is the process of taking action.**

If you have not noticed, humankind is mainly composed of doers. Doing is what most people are focused on during their lives. I find there is a consistent unified message that is being broadcast by those who have a particular worldview that our value is about our performance, positive outcomes or actions. This message is highly effective and is being heard and acted upon by people worldwide.

All you need to do is look around you at everything made by men and women. We are being told and reinforced to believe, that we live in a competitive world based on limited resources. To survive, one must compete. We learn early in our lives that the world values certain things, and people want to be recognized as winners, which means some people must lose since there are not enough resources to go around.

Even though some individuals in this world have gone to great lengths to modify history to meet their agenda, there are still some people who know there was a time in recent history when the world looked vastly different. It has only been in the last hundred and fifty years or so that the doing of humans has profoundly changed the face of our globe, seemingly forever. These changes I must point out are not all positive and will likely continue if something different is not offered and accepted.

It is evident to me, and I hope to you: we are life forms of action. We imagine, we plan, and we create through our actions.

Unfortunately, this constant doing has become a compulsion that has become a form of mental and emotional torment for many. This is partly because of the way our brains are wired. What is repetitively done over and over becomes stronger and stronger.

If we take specific actions continually, they become automatic, and the harder it is for us to find balance in our lives, which we require if we want to be healthy. **I would propose that *doing* has become an end in itself rather than a means to an end. That is why we can never find ultimate satisfaction in doing alone.**

Points and questions you may want to ponder:

What was the doing in the story, "What Friendship?," that you think was right or wrong to do?

Instincts

> Instincts are the innate set of possible reactions used by people to survive and are chosen automatically by one's brain.

You have already learned that the primary function of our brain is survival. Now, let us look at the source of instincts. Instincts have been passed down from generation to generation, beginning with the first human being on Earth. This will likely continue until the last humans take their last breath.

Instincts always have good intentions for their host. However, in life, it takes more than simply good intentions, as you know. **Even with the best intentions, our instincts can get us into trouble. They are ancient in origin. It is precisely this characteristic that can be problematic for all human beings.** Given our current living environment, circumstances, and the context most of us find ourselves operating in, there is a real inconsistency between our instincts and how effectively we use them to assist us in our quest for survival.

You cannot talk about human instincts without mentioning the human brain as we currently understand it. The instinctual part of our brain is at the rear of our heads. It is the oldest part of our brain. It gets the information first and is sometimes known as the reptilian brain.[22] Think of this part as an autopilot on a plane. When engaged, it takes over and reacts without you doing anything. It says, "I got it from here." The problem is that instincts are not always in the best interest of the individual.

---

[22] Hjelle, Larry; Ziegler, Daniel (1981). Personality Theories: Basic Assumptions, Research, and Applications. McGraw-Hill. p. 494. ISBN 9780070290631. Is this about the reptilian brain?

Just because our brains perceive a threat does not mean danger exists.

In my private practice, I see people in survival mode and driven by their instincts. Many do not understand how or why they are in that state. They just know they are emotionally hurting and are unclear about what action to take to improve their lives. Most of them have tried all other options before trying counseling. I am glad they finally made it to the right place. I am sad they had to go through so much pain before they got here. I often do my best to reassure them that they have finally arrived at the right place and now is the time to figure it out.

My experience teaches me this: people often do not know there is someone out there who can provide real help. They keep trying to do it by themselves until they cannot handle the situation any longer. When people come to see me, I wish I could take some pictures or video clips to show you the condition of people when they enter my office and when they are done with their scheduled session (the before and after). It is evident when the weight of the world has been lifted off their shoulders. I look forward to seeing it each time I meet with those who come to see me. They come in one way and leave my office better than they could ever have imagined in many ways.

You already know human beings have instincts, but do you know you do not have to be submissive or controlled by all of them all of the time? You have the newest part of your brain to help you; however, it is the least developed in most humans. It is your prefrontal lobe. It is located behind your forehead. This part of your brain is also known as your executive center.[30] This is the part

---

[30] Bettcher, B. M., Mungas, D. M., Patel, N., Elofson, J., Dutt, S., Wynn, M. J., Watson, C., Stephens, M., Walsh, C. A., & Kramer, J. H. (2016). Neuroanatomical substrates of executive functions: Beyond prefrontal structures. Neuropsychologia, 85, 100–109. https://doi.org/10.1016/j.neuropsychologia.2016.03.001.

of your brain in which logic wins based on the weighing of facts. It is about the big picture and what is best, considering as much as possible. It takes time for this part of your brain to be activated, and it is not used as often as our instincts when the brain thinks it is in real danger.

Let me give you an example. Let us say you are outdoors at a national park, and you see something far away, so you must use binoculars for the first time in your life. As you will learn when you look through binoculars, you see things as much larger because the image is magnified. If your brain only sees a bear that appears to be right in front of you, it will react with "Red Light, Danger, Danger!" and you might even jump back or run away. That would be an example of your instincts being triggered because your brain perceiving a real threat. Now, in this case, the bear is a mile away. There is no real danger, so there is no need to jump back or run away. This is a rather simplistic example, but I hope it makes my point.

You already know, as awesome as it is, your brain can make mistakes and does so regularly when it comes to real threats and dangers. There are many ways our brain can get tripped up when it comes to our instincts. If you want to learn more, I encourage you to do so. It is a fascinating area to explore.

Points and questions you may want to ponder:

In the story "What Friendship?", identify Wanda's instincts.

Do you think she did the right thing given what had happened to her?

Passivity

> Passivity is the lack of taking action—no matter what—when others do something that affects you.

Not a week goes by when someone does not tell me what they do not like about their lives. I continue to choose to experience this because it is so rewarding for me to have the privilege of offering what I can to assist others within limits. This is how I am made and who I have chosen to become: someone who lives life as authentically as possible. I use the word *possible* because I am a work in progress.

Have you ever thought about how not acting in some situations is worse than acting? If not, perhaps it is time you did. Today there are many challenges we face all over the world. If we are to solve them, each of us must do our part and work together constructively. This includes you and is part of the reason I am writing this book. I want to help as many people as I can to be free of unnecessary limitations.

Being free comes with a big responsibility. Responsibility is designed to help motivate us to take constructive action. I believe in leaving the world better in some way than I found it. You may know many people who follow others blindly or follow those who speak the loudest or have the most friends or followers who agree with them. **It is true—often, the majority rules; however, this does not guarantee the majority is right and just.** It could be that they have bad intentions and are very wrong. Sometimes, being passive is necessary, but it is not a state to be in all of one's life.

You cannot be passive all the time if you intend to make a difference in this world. You are needed even if you do not know what you can do. I am asking you not to quit or give up on life right now. In the short term, I know it may be easier to bury one's head in the sand and escape reality by going to one's happy place. I also know that whatever you do not confront, you cannot change.[31] Often, it takes more than just your desire to stand up for yourself and what you believe. I am here to help you, and I am sure that there are others out there too. I hope you will agree there is a fundamental difference between right and wrong, and right still matters a lot in one's life!

The point I am trying to make here is that when you can, connect with like-minded people who are on the side of right and then do your part. The alternative is to sit on the sidelines, complain, and watch the world as you know it slip away into darkness. I have discovered that if you do not step up and be counted, others will step in and make decisions for you, and you will become just another blind follower. This is the only world we have now, and when it is gone, so are we. I hope this is not too much reality for you. I am just trying to keep it real.

Points and questions you may want to ponder:

Based on what you know and have learned about passivity in the story, do you think Wanda was too passive?

---

[31] oprahzipbradford.com/2019/11/20/you-cant-change-what-you-refuse-to-confront/.

Empathy

> Empathy is imagining what others may be going through mentally and emotionally by putting yourself in their place.

You may be aware that there are multiple types of intelligence. Many people know about IQ or intelligence quotient, where the average IQ is around 100 in most developed countries.[32] I want to point out another kind of intelligence known as emotional intelligence (EQ), which is rated on a number scale too. The average EQ score is between 90 and 100 in most developed countries, out of a possible 160.[33] Emotional intelligence involves emotion, and empathy is a part of the overall EQ equation.

I have found that empathy varies a great deal from one person to another. The big challenge I see in my practice in relationship counseling occurs when one person seems not to have the same empathy level as their partner. This can create a lot of misunderstanding, which can ultimately result in the termination of that relationship. It is often extremely hard for people, in general, to understand that a person can have an extremely high IQ, and at the same time, have an incredibly low EQ. People commonly assume that IQ really covers EQ; this assumption is wrong. They are two different forms of intelligence.

There is a way to improve one's empathy, and it involves reducing negative thoughts. Negative thoughts about a person will minimize any possibility of having much empathy toward that person.

---

[32] Braaten, Ellen B.; Norman, Dennis (1 November 2006). "Intelligence (IQ) Testing". Pediatrics in Review. 27 (11): 403–408. doi:10.1542/pir.27-11-403. ISSN 0191-9601. Retrieved 21 May 2020.

[33] Mayer, J. E., Caruso, D. R., & Salovey, P. (1999). Emotional intelligence meets traditional standards for an intelligence. Intelligence, 27(4), 267–298.

When a person is dealing with their own emotional pain, it is unrealistic to expect them to be very empathetic. It is just not going to happen.

Sometimes, in my sessions, one member of the coupleship will attempt to share their pain openly with the other member, and the response from the other member will be, "What about me?" When I hear this, I know it may be helpful to meet with them individually, so they can work on themselves before I can help them with their relationship any further.

Points and questions you may want to ponder:

In the story "What Friendship?", do you think Wanda's landlord had much empathy?

What do you think was keeping Wanda from having a better life?

Life-Changing Learning Opportunities

Please pause for a moment and list some of your thoughts and feelings from what you have just experienced. After doing this, I recommend you write down the actions you will take to affect your future for the better. Do this based on what comes first to your mind after reading the story with its accompanying foundational human knowledge.

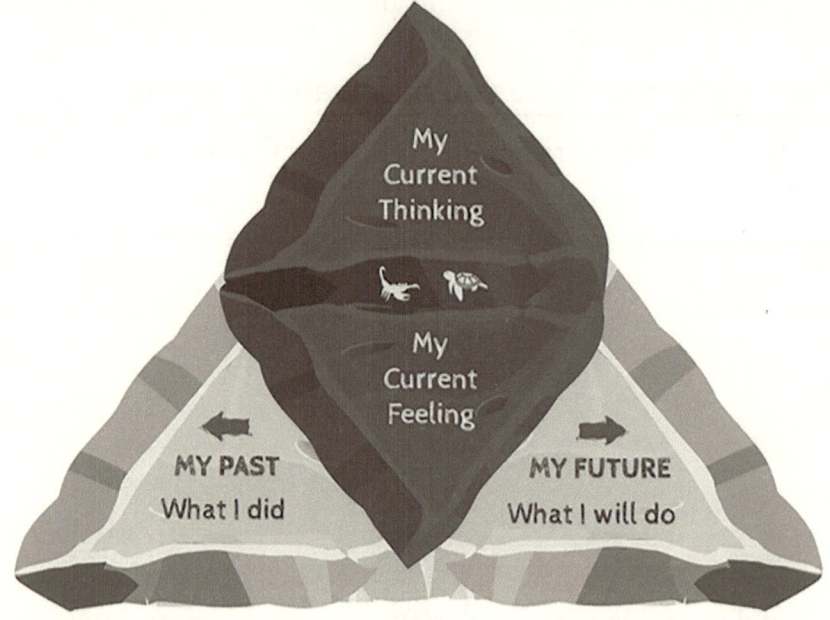

Figure 16: Life-Changing Learning Opportunities Pyramid

My Additional Current Thoughts

My Current Feelings

Actions That Will Affect My Future

CHAPTER THIRTEEN

A ONE-WAY TICKET

Betrayal Story

Brenda came to see me one Saturday morning. She began our time together with the question, "Where do I start?"

I assured her that wherever she felt like starting would be good. She said she grew up in a regular middle-class family most of her early years, and her parents got divorced when she started high school. Because of this, she and her younger brother were shuttled between her father part of the time and her mother the rest of the time. It seemed to her that her younger brother was able to manage all the changes better than she could. She thought this because her brother finished school and found a good job helping humankind by finding better ways to recycle human trash, and married a wonderful woman.

On the other hand, Brenda was still single, thirty years old, and had never had a relationship that lasted more than seven or eight months. I asked her why she thought that was. She said, "I am not able to trust men because they are all the same." She continued after a brief pause and explained she had been an airline flight attendant for most of her career. She asked if I knew much about what often happens in the airline business. I responded with, "I only fly from time to time."

She said, "I am not talking about flying; I am talking about the lifestyle." She went on to provide me with an example. Once she had fallen in love with a man only to find out some six months after they met, he was married and had five kids. Of course, that was something he had failed to mention when he was telling her that he was falling in love with her and was considering what it would be like to spend the rest of his life with her.

She finished with, "That is why I think all men are alike. You cannot trust them, and I am starting to hate them because they will always break your heart."

It was clear to both of us that Brenda had more to share. We only had an hour scheduled that day, and we had already gone a little over our time, so we agreed to meet again in a week and pick up where she had left off. She thanked me for being a good listener. Since it was after dark, I walked with her from my office to where she could exit the building next to the parking lot and stood there watching her until she got in her car safely and drove off.

Who is who?

Who had scorpion-like behaviors? _____

Who had turtle-like behaviors? _____

FOUNDATIONAL HUMAN KNOWLEDGE

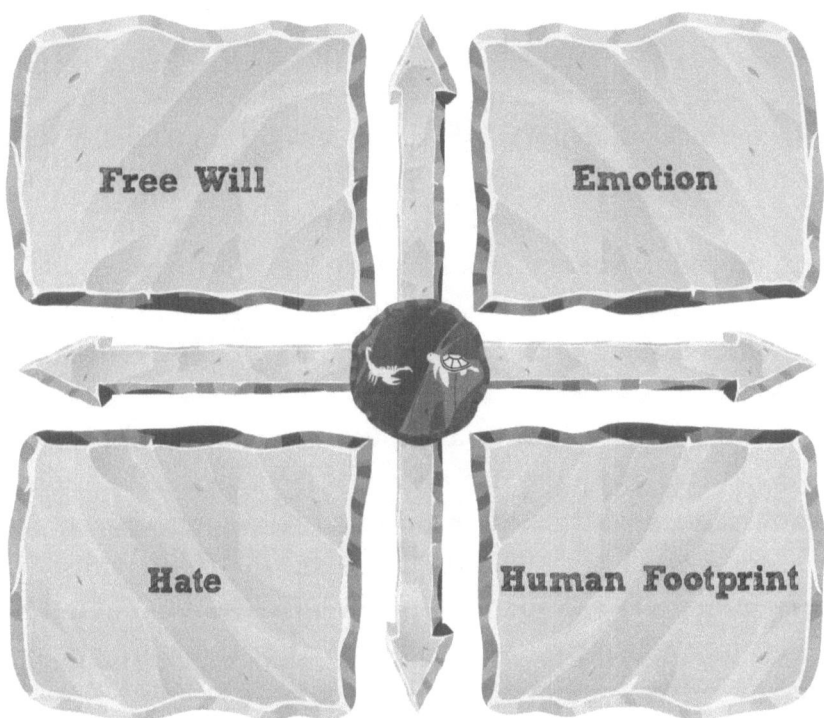

Figure 17: Chapter Thirteen - Foundational Human Knowledge

Free Will

> **Free will is having the freedom to choose one's actions from available possibilities.**

Do you know free will is never free? There is always a cost to having freedom. Free will is not a right of humanity. Free will is not a guarantee. Freedom of will carries with it a high price and a great deal of responsibility. Over my lifetime, I have seen many people take the privilege of having free will for granted. People seem to be so careless concerning their free will. We live in an age when people aggregate together to create a large, powerful, focused mass that thinks alike and takes action to get what they want from others. Riots and wars are happening in many countries around the world as of the writing of this book, which displays this mass thinking.

I find this process to be hazardous for the future of humanity. I believe the very existence of free will is at risk. Immediate action is required from all of us if it is to be preserved in any way, form, or fashion. **To protect the future of humanity, we must preserve the option to think for ourselves and not follow others just because we want to be a part of something bigger than ourselves.**

There are many examples in our recent history of people who blindly followed others, which resulted in great harm to millions of people who no longer have a future. Their lack of a future negatively affects all of us, whether we realize it or not. Many scientists and others seem divided concerning the existence of a free will. Many of them do not believe free will exists.[34] They think we are a product of our environment and genetics, and

---

[34] Omoregie, J. (2015). *Free Will: The Degree of Freedom Within.*

there is nothing else. I am not one of those people. I believe in the uniqueness of each human being.

Science has a hard time proving the existence or nonexistence of free will. In our so-called modern society, we learn to believe much of what we know and accept as the truth from science. There seems to be a rather popular position held by many in our current world that if it is not scientific, then it is not valid. Let me give you one example that is not necessarily scientific, but I believe is true nonetheless. It seems most legal systems around the world assume people have a level of free will, and they are specific concerning what negative consequences there are for people making bad decisions. Therefore, according to society, free will exists whether science has proven it or not.

My position on free will is that we have some level of it. It is shaped by internal and external factors, which will never negate our responsibility to ourselves and others to use it wisely. I find we frequently make decisions on what we think works best for us. I am okay with this reasoning up to the point it does not harm others unnecessarily. I am all about win-win!

Points and questions you may want to ponder:

How did Brenda demonstrate her free will in the story "Betrayal"?

Emotion

> Emotion is the way in which humans ultimately experience life by perceiving something as positive or negative through their feelings.

The event's specific significance determines the specific quality of the emotion (e.g., fear, shame). For example, if a person perceives a threat, fear will likely to be generated. If it involves disapproval from another, shame is likely to be generated.

I see, primarily two types of people in my practice. One type is about what they think, and the other is about what they feel. I believe it is essential if you want to have the best life possible to develop both and use them as needed. Please allow me to provide you with a couple of statements followed by a powerful learning example. As a living human being, one is required to survive, and we must learn everything, as you know. Then one might ask, what is the best way to understand something that will enable you to survive? The example that follows is designed to help you define what would help you the most to learn from this experience. This example involves thinking (reasoning only) versus feeling. For instance, let us say you are being introduced to a hot stove for the first time and have no prior knowledge about it. A person shows you a hot burner on the hot stove and tells you the red ring on the stove is a burner, and it is red hot and will burn you if you were to put your hand on it. You would be in a lot of pain depending on how much time you left it there. That is the only information you have. What do you think you would understand and learn from this approach by only using your reasoning?

Okay, let us do this again, but this time, you are told to put your right hand on the same red-hot stove burner for only four seconds. Which approach do you think would help you the most to understand and learn what a hot stove burner is? I am going to take a wild guess. It is an example of when you would hypothetically put your hand on the red-hot stove burner. I think you know why, too. It was that you not only engaged your reasoning but you also experienced it through your emotions in the form of pain. In this example, your emotions were your best teacher. In this example, experiencing life through your emotions was painful. I find this can often be the case. Some of you may be asking yourself if emotions can be painful, then I will just shut down my feelings and only use my reasoning and take my chances in life.

If I may, I would like to share another personal story. I lived in a rural community called Ocklawaha, which is now close to The Villages, for most of my early years. I am an only child. Other than interacting with others of my age during school, my primary interaction was with adults. Looking back, I can see I grew up too fast. One of the challenges I had as a child was experiencing my own emotions and the emotions of others. There was a period in my life when if I could have eliminated emotions, I would have. The reason for this desire to eliminate my emotions revolved around primarily experiencing negative emotions and the hurt and pain that go along with them. As a child, I thought that if I were to eliminate my emotions, I could stop my pain, so I began to shut them down. I am confident I had good intentions. I did not realize that I created other problems that I had not anticipated by reducing or shutting down my emotions. I began to adopt a strategy of preparing for the worst, so I could not be disappointed or hurt any more than I already was.

It has not been just my own experience but also my experience in private practice that this process of **shutting down one's**

emotions for any real length of time is dangerous, as I stated earlier in this book. You may recall this is because it shuts down both the negative possibilities and the possibilities of experiencing life in a positive manner as well. This can create a solution that is worse than the original problem! Do you know of anyone who has numbed themselves or tried to escape from their negative emotions? I thought you might. It has taken me a while and a lot of deliberate work, but I have finally turned this around. Now, I can see life more fully and experience life more as it actually is, the good, the bad, and the ugly. This positive shift in how I deal with my emotions has been responsible for a real improvement in my quality of life. If you choose to give it a try, I think it will in your life as well.

Points and questions you may want to ponder:

What were some of Brenda's emotions?

Have you ever shut down your emotions for a period of time?

Hate

> Hate is an extremely negative emotion based on one or more feelings generated from thoughts such as dislike and contempt, often with anger, which creates beliefs that are the opposite of love.

During my lifetime, I have noticed a disturbing trend around the world toward people filling themselves with hate for others and even themselves. Hate is very destructive for the person generating it and the person who may be at the receiving end. Hate only destroys and leaves no winners. The person with hate inside them is producing chemicals in their own body that can slowly kill them.[35] I believe we are not meant to hate, which is why it is so destructive both internally to our bodies and externally to our relationships and environment. If you pay attention to today's news, you will see repeated examples of how people around the world are using hate as motivation and justification for their actions of creating harm.

It is my observation that once people begin to hate, their hatred seems to feed on itself and grows and grows until it consumes the person. That is all they can think about day after day until something gives. We all know of countries that have been fighting each other for years; their justification is based on hatred. This hatred continues from one generation to another, nonstop. **I believe there is a high probability that humanity is at an evolutionary tipping point.**[36] **It may now be easier for us to hate than to love.**

---

[35] Zeki et al. Neural Correlates of Hate. PLoS ONE, 2008; 3 (10): e3556 DOI: 10.1371/journal.pone.0003556.

[36] Matthew M. Osmond, Christopher A. Klausmeier, An evolutionary tipping point in a changing environment, Evolution, Volume 71, Issue 12, 1 December 2017, Pages 2930–2941, https://doi.org/10.1111/evo.13374

I pray each day that this is not the case. Hate uses up so many of the resources of a country. Many countries' gross domestic product (GDP) revenue pays for their military expenses for self-protection from those who hate them and seek to destroy them.[37] Can you think of better ways to spend the money we could save if we were not in wars or preparing for future wars? I can think of many!

Please understand me; I am not against self-protection. It is just that I am not in favor of justifying one's actions using hate as a motivating factor to hurt oneself or others. I wonder what the world would be like if we all got up tomorrow and there was no more hate, and human beings could hate no more in the future?

Points and questions you may want to ponder:

What effect did the emotion of hate have on Brenda in the story?

Do you have any hate in your heart that you know is not helpful?

---

[37] https://www.theglobaleconomy.com/rankings/mil_spend_gdp/.

Human Footprint

> Human footprint is the effect human beings are having and have had on themselves and this planet.

The real problem is that human beings have a challenge in the area of their lives known as ownership. This process begins early in the life of a young child who utters the words "mine, mine, mine," all the time. It appears we like to take possession; hence, we own and have things.[38] I believe this is built into our design and experiences of wanting and sometimes having, or wanting and not having, reinforced in us from early life. You already know that, as good as our brain is at helping each of us, it is not perfect.

Our brains often get confused about understanding the difference between wanting and needing. What once used to be desired has now become required. I have witnessed over the years a real blurring of the lines. Early in my life, I observed unfiltered children who were not yet fully socialized refer to what they wanted as "I want."

As I stated earlier in this book, it is not uncommon for me today to observe both children and adults who no longer talk about what they need, but rather only make statements of "I want." If I did not know better, I would think there was no such thing as need anymore, and there was only want. Many people now see every want as a critical requirement for survival. Given that we are born and made to seek survival, it seems reasonable that owning is a form of control, and that which we control helps us feel more secure. This leads us to continue seeking and buying more things.

---

[38] https://maximizeminimalism.com/7-reasons-why-people-are-obsessed-material-possessions/.

As a result, we become more and more psychologically and emotionally attached to never getting or having enough of anything, including pain. At this stage, a few of you may be asking yourselves, what does this have to do with the *human footprint*? My answer is, it has a lot to do with how we humans approach everything we encounter.

This includes how we affect all living things on this planet and any planet we may go to if we do not evolve past this limitation. Because humans are driven by their instincts and must own and possess, they must seek to control to satisfy their need to feel more secure. Once these things are better understood, our history and current situation as a species begin to make a lot more sense.

Anywhere I focus my attention, I observe human beings who struggle with one another over ownership. All one must do is look at the creation of countless laws humanity has created that involve one's rights, including the right of ownership. As we know, our physical brains are not evolving as quickly as society and technology are moving.

There was a time in my youth when people took pride and cared for what little they owned because they valued it so greatly. It seems we are not living in those times anymore. We are now living in a world in which things are made, and when they no longer work to our satisfaction, as we would like, they become disposable. This change in the easy disposal of items also includes people. **If our actions speak for what is in our hearts and minds, many human beings do not care anymore about how they affect each other, this planet, and all the life it supports.**

This implies our world has become disposable. I am not saying this is the viewpoint of all human beings, and to this end, I am very thankful and optimistic that much can be done to correct the harmful effects of human footprints on our planet and each other. If this is going to happen, each of us must rise above our instincts and work in cooperation with one another for the good of the many. Yes, I know this may mean that we may not have all we want in life, but it could mean we could have all we need. This is so much better than disappearing as a life form.

I hope you will agree with me!

Points and questions you may want to ponder:

In the story "Betrayal", in what way was the human footprint significant to Brenda?

Do you think Brenda had what she wanted in life?

Life-Changing Learning Opportunities

Please pause for a moment and list some of your thoughts and feelings from what you have just experienced. After doing this, I recommend you write down the actions you will take to affect your future for the better. Do this based on what comes first to your mind after reading the story with its accompanying foundational human knowledge.

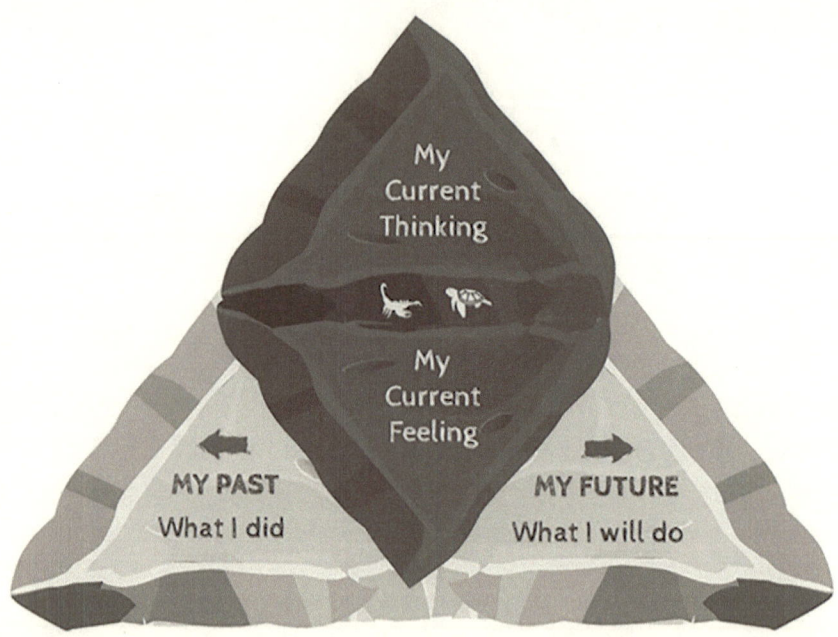

Figure 18: Life-Changing Learning Opportunities Pyramid

My Additional Current Thoughts

My Current Feelings

Actions That Will Affect My Future

CHAPTER FOURTEEN

DEATH AND DIVORCE

Confused Story

Not long ago, in my office I met with a couple who were professionals in their chosen fields of study. They came to see me for marriage counseling. The woman was in her mid-forties, and her new husband was fifteen years younger than her. This was the second marriage for both. After settling down in my office for a three-hour session, I began by asking each of them what had brought them to see me. What follows is some of what happened. The woman began by telling me she met her new husband in the local hospital where they both worked, about two years before, when she was still married to her first husband, and one thing led to another. She had been unhappily married for the previous five years of her then ten-year marriage. She was going to divorce her husband, but he died in an auto accident before she could file the papers.

Then her current husband of only ten months asked if he could say something. He began by saying, "When I met this woman over there, I was also married." He seemed rather angry and went on to say he had divorced his first wife to be with his new wife, and he did not believe she would have followed through and divorced her first husband had he not died. He also said, "All she wants is sex; I mean all the time, like five times a day."

The woman looked at me and said, "I am guilty. Just look at him—he is in great shape. I can't get enough of him." She did not say anything about her willingness to get a divorce while she was still married to her first husband. Speaking of her current husband, she went on to say their fights began over the prenuptial, which was an absolute nightmare! "Dr. Bill, it was as if we were going through a divorce already. He kept saying if I loved him, I would be willing to give him half of everything I had if, for some reason, we did not stay married."

The woman explained she had been working for many years as a physician, and not only had she made a lot of money for herself, but most recently after her first husband's death. She had inherited a great deal more because he had come from a very wealthy family that had always taken excellent care of him. The remainder of the three-hour session was regarding her money.

Finally, I said, "Tell me if I am wrong, but it appears to me there are some real trust issues here." At this point, the wife spoke up. "I think a lot of it has to do with how we met and that we were both married at the same time we saw each other. We know what each of us is capable of, and I am not sure, after a few years, when I am older and have put on some weight, that my husband would not one day say he is done with me."

Her husband could not stand being quiet any longer, so he interrupted by saying, "Really, I do not trust you either. Dr. Bill, she is already saying I am only after her money. I think what she likes about being with me is how much sex she can have and how she is seen when we go out."

I moved my chair forward and said, "I think it is safe to say, given we have already gone three hours, that everyone is getting tired, and I do not think we can resolve all the issues in one meeting. I am suggesting we wrap up for now, but before we do, I want to provide each of you the opportunity to say anything you would like to say before we end our time together today."

The man was the first to respond: "I know we have our fights, but I do love my wife."

I said, "You love your wife?"

He said, "Yes, I do."

I looked over to his wife and said, "Did you hear that?"

She said, "I did, and I love my husband too, which is why I married him in the first place instead of marrying anyone else. He was not the only option I had, after all."

After her statement, we all got up from our chairs, and I moved out of my office through the main door first. I thought they were right behind me, but I was wrong. I stepped back to see into my office through the open door and was pleasantly surprised at what I saw. I observed them in the middle of a warm embrace. I waited a few minutes. They came out of the office together, holding hands, thanking me, and saying they both wanted to come back to work on their marriage further.

I replied with, "Absolutely!" I did see them a few more times, and each of them on separate meetings as well. It has now been over ten years since I have had any contact with either of them. Most people, once they get help, move on with their lives. I do not hear from them until they need my assistance again. I have learned to accept this, even though I wonder how they are doing.

Who is who?

Who had scorpion-like behaviors? _____

Who had turtle-like behaviors? _____

FOUNDATIONAL HUMAN KNOWLEDGE

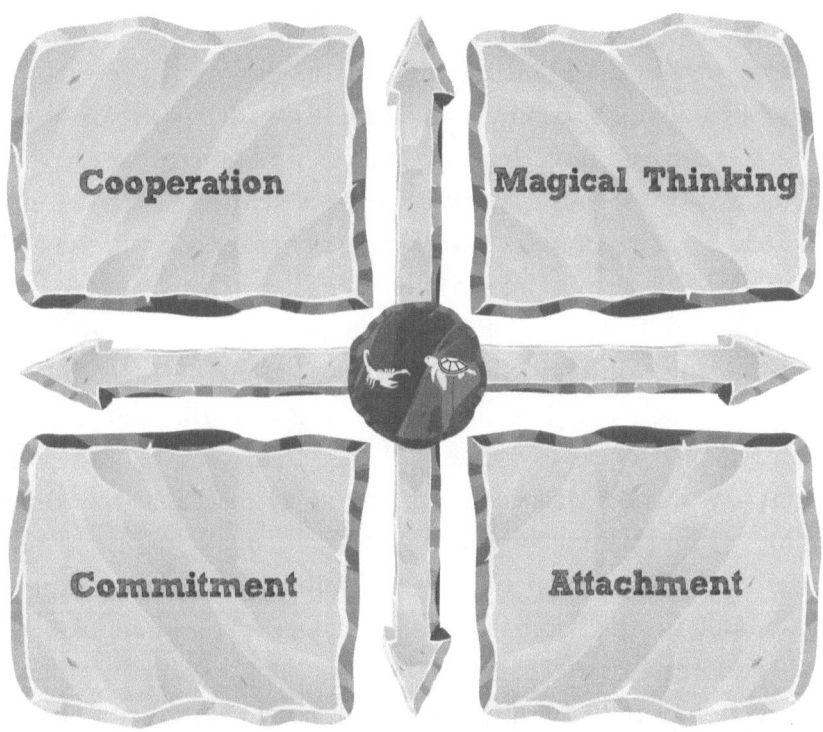

Figure 19: Chapter Fourteen - Foundational Human Knowledge

Cooperation

> **Cooperation is an action a person takes to work together for the good of themselves and others.**

What does cooperation have to do with anything? If you were alone on this planet, then it would not matter much. Since most people are not alone on this planet, the answer is everything! **The one constant thing we all share is our drive for survival, and some of us have learned that if we want prosperity it is necessary to cooperate with others around us.** If we do not learn to cooperate better with one another, we will see the probability of our extinction increase. That makes cooperation rather important! Have you ever considered why you were born and how the world got to where it is now? I have.

Many nights as a young child, I sat on the end of my grandparents' dock overlooking Lake Weir, looking into the night sky, wondering why I was here in this place at this time in history and why the world was as it is. One night I heard the song "Stairway to Heaven" coming from the dark lake. I knew it was not coming from Eaton's Beach across the other side of the lake because the music was too clear. I could only hear clear music from what was then Johnson's Beach, now Gator Joe's, because they were less than a quarter mile away and invited recording artists and bands to play during the summer months on weekends. Living in the country, I had a lot of free time to ponder such things. It took me many nights before I figured out some answers to my questions. I concluded that living at this time in this place was not by some random act or event; there must be some purpose to it all. I know I am not alone in asking such questions.

The great minds of science are now beginning to recognize how rare you and I are and what we are capable of in life. The question is, "What are each of us going to do with this rare gift of life?" We can choose to live it selfishly, only thinking of ourselves, or live it with the intention of making the world a better place than we found it. The latter requires us to cooperate with others toward common goals that are good for this planet and humanity.

There is so much struggle in this world. I believe much of it is self-imposed. Many people seem to have a rebellious attitude or do not care very much about others. The root of this is that they no longer care about themselves. It is impossible to care about others without first caring about yourself. I have touched on this previously. In my office, I regularly remind couples who are having trouble finding ways to appreciate and love one another that cooperation is about two or more people having a desire to do something together for their mutual benefit. I sometimes see one or both acting as if they want cooperation, but it is often only about their own best interest. This is especially true if they are in scorpion-like mode and not thinking of anyone else, and they cooperate only to get what they want. When that is over, their cooperation ends as well.

Points and questions you may want to ponder:

Was there any genuine cooperation between the couple in the story "Confused"?

What reasons for cooperation could have been solely about the person, and what part could have been about the coupleship for each of them?

Do you think this relationship will last?

Magical Thinking

> Magical thinking is the unrealistic belief in what creates positive or negative outcomes based on something other than truth.

Let me start with another example from my own life. You never forget certain things as a parent, and one of those things for me has to do with my son, Jon-Austin Singer, who was around four years old at the time. Living in Orlando, with all the theme parks, is very convenient when you want to get out of the house and have some real fun together.

On one particularly hot and humid summer day, I spent most of the day and evening with a friend and my son at one of the largest theme parks in the area. I will tell you, if you do not know, that four-year-olds have an incredible amount of energy. I spent most of my time trying to keep up with him. As the day turned into evening, I was doing all I could to keep at least one eye open while my son was still going strong. One of the things you do at large theme parks is walk, walk, and walk some more.

While walking from one part of the park to another, I realized my son was not right next to me when I looked down at my side. As a parent, I tried not to panic, but this was alarming. I immediately retraced my steps. In about five seconds, which seemed like an eternity, I found him standing by some flowers. I came up behind him, and I could hear him saying something to himself. I moved a little closer until I could make out what he was saying. He was pulling the petals off a small flower he had picked and reciting a nursery rhyme he had learned in preschool.

When I could not stand it any longer, I announced myself and asked him what he was doing. He said with a certain tone and a look as if to say, *Is it not rather obvious, Dad! I am trying to make a decision.* Being the good doctor that I am, I said, "Oh!" Then, I tried logic and offered him an alternative, which he promptly discarded.

The main point I want to make here is that he was using magical thinking to try to find a solution to his problem at the age of four. This may be reasonable for a four-year-old, but it would not be for a sixteen-year-old who was about to get their driver's license or for an adult. As human beings, we are constantly being influenced by something or someone. This is part of our learning process.

The challenge comes when we must use what we have learned to navigate through life. **There are adults still using magical thinking to solve problematic or difficult situations that affect their lives.** They have not learned that it takes much more than this type of fantasy thinking to resolve problems in a real world as complex as the one we find ourselves living in. If you know you are a person caught up in make-believe and trying to avoid the "real world," I would ask you to consider reaching out to a behavioral health professional who will not judge you but help you begin to reconnect with life around you as it actually is. I know there may be many reasons you have chosen to try to escape. All I am asking is that you would give some real thought to re-engagement.

Points and questions you may want to ponder:

What magical thinking was present in the story "Confused" above?

Who had magical thinking? Do you think it was helpful?

Commitment

> **Commitment means I will or I will not, period. When you make a commitment, it means you must dedicate yourself to something or someone.**

Please think carefully before committing to anything, because it obligates you to do something. Some commitments are significant, like marriage.

I see many people who are in conflict and are having difficulty with commitment. They are going through the motions of daily life without committing to a plan regarding how to live it. Some may have vague goals, but they have never put them down in writing. Others have no goals other than trying to do whatever they want in life by pursuing pleasure and avoiding pain as much as possible. I find people do better in life overall if they believe in something they can commit to during their lives. The world today, led by certain human beings, is in a real crisis.

Everywhere you look, people are afraid and have real health concerns. There are wars, environmental problems, poverty, and inequality, all driven by political and financial uncertainties. We have become people who spend our precious time focusing on our differences, no matter the consequences. This conflict is further dividing this world and destroying people from the inside out. The stress that the average person is experiencing is reaching critical mass.

Regularly, I talk with people who are experiencing such extreme levels of stress that they are ill. I am not only referring to mental and emotional illness but physical illness as well. I see people who are in jobs they do not like and even hate, and in relationships or marriages in which one or both people are not committed and are using the other as a means to an end. This is causing so much pain and destruction in our world today.

I often wonder how humans, who are supposed to be the highest life forms on this planet, have so much trouble making and keeping commitments when, for example, other lower life forms keep their commitments for life.

Here, to name just a few, are some of these so-called lower life forms—all of them are birds—that commit to their mates for life: mallard ducks, penguins, black vultures, bald eagles, scarlet macaw, whooping crane, California condor, and Atlantic puffin. Even when one in a pair dies, most of them will not look for another partner.[39] How is this possible? I do not know. Nevertheless, I know it is true. I think we humans could learn a lot from them.

I believe humans are less committed to one another than ever before because we are less committed to *anything* in this world. I wonder how long this will last before it is game over.

You might be asking, "So, what can one do?". My experience teaches me that it is important to believe first in *Truth* and commit to taking positive action. **All of us can look around and find a small part of this world we can be a part of commit our lives and resources. Each of us can commit to improving it, not only for ourselves but also for the generations to come.** When I use the word *commit*, I mean we go all in! Not just when it is convenient or when we are having a good time but staying committed all the time, for better or worse. That is what commitment truly is.

I think it would be better for us all to stop complaining about life and start doing something about the challenges that affect all of us. Let me encourage you to commit and then act on it by

---

[39] https://www.audubon.org/news/till-death-do-them-part-8-birds-mate-life

doing your part to make this world better than it is right now! Some of you already believe something. You may believe this world is hopeless, and you are helpless to do anything about it. Coming from a loving place, I must let you know that you have a false belief. It is not over yet. You have something only you can offer. Now is the time; there is no do-over. This world needs you. Please get involved and help us all!

Points and questions you may want to ponder:

Do you think the couple in the story "Confused" was committed to their relationship?

Attachment

> Attachment is the emotional and psychological bond that often forms between a child and who cares for it. It helps children get their primary needs met. It can be a strong connection to places and things as well as ideas and beliefs.

If you have an attachment to someone or something, you feel more secure because trust is built.

Attachment can be an act or a process. It is bonding with someone or something else. It can denote a strong dependence on something or someone.

I will attempt to shed some light on attachment for you from several points of view. One will be from psychology, and the other I will draw from my own experiences.

Attachment begins at our first breath and is either formed or not by two years of age.[40] In psychology, this is better known as the attachment theory.[41] There is much to be said concerning this theory. Let me give you the highlights. When a person is born, there is a bond they develop or not develop due to caregiving from their primary care giver. This bond is essential to each human being because it can negatively affect the child's life throughout adulthood if it is not formed in healthy ways. A healthy bond allows the child to feel emotionally safe and continue developing because they get all their survival needs and some of their higher-level needs met, including loving

---

[40] Hong YR, Park JS. Impact of attachment, temperament and parenting on human development. Korean J Pediatr. 2012 Dec;55(12):449-54. doi: 10.3345/kjp.2012.55.12.449. Epub 2012 Dec 20. PMID: 23300499; PMCID: PMC3534157.

[41] https://www.simplypsychology.org/attachment.html.

touch. I suspect you are aware that not everyone is brought up the same way around the world, leading to different forms of attachment or the lack thereof.

Healthy attachment is based on trust. If the child cannot trust their caregiver during this critical time in their lives, they will develop different forms of attachments, which will most likely continue into the rest of their lives. This may be why some people bond with their mates for life while others cannot. Some people will only let you get so close to them emotionally, no matter how long you are with them or what you may offer to them.

They are simply not fully available! I hope you now better understand how attachment not only affects our relationships but also our entire lives. Let us turn our attention to other forms of attachment and their relationships to emotional pain. From my experience, and I suspect yours, it is no secret that there is a great deal of emotional pain in the world. You might be asking why there is so much. Would you like to be let in on another secret? I believe much of one's emotional pain can be reduced if one decides to do so. When I say *decides*, you may be asking, "Does this mean that emotional pain is only a choice?" No, but much of life's emotional pain can be avoided, and what cannot be avoided often can be reduced by the deliberate decisions you make.

Now, I said it! I work with many people who have attached the sense of who they are to what they do for a living, where they were born, who their parents were, their school, skin color, age, and gender. These are all forms of attachment.

I am not suggesting that you form attachments by choice only. What I am suggesting is that you can choose the importance you place on your attachments and thus to what degree you value them. This becomes your connection and thus your attachment to them. Here comes the real secret. If you are not attached to them, they cannot hurt you emotionally. This is where you are empowered to make decisions concerning how they will affect you in your life. If what you are experiencing is positive, then enjoy! If it is negative, consider casting it off and being done with it! The choice, in the end, is yours to make. I am in no way saying it is easy to let go of negative attachments. It can be done in many situations if you get the right kind of support and guidance.

Points and questions you may want to ponder:

Do you think attachment was an issue for the couple in the story "Confused"?

Life-Changing Learning Opportunities

Please pause for a moment and list some of your thoughts and feelings from what you have just experienced. After doing this, I recommend you write down the actions you will take to affect your future for the better. Do this based on what comes first to your mind after reading the story with its accompanying foundational human knowledge.

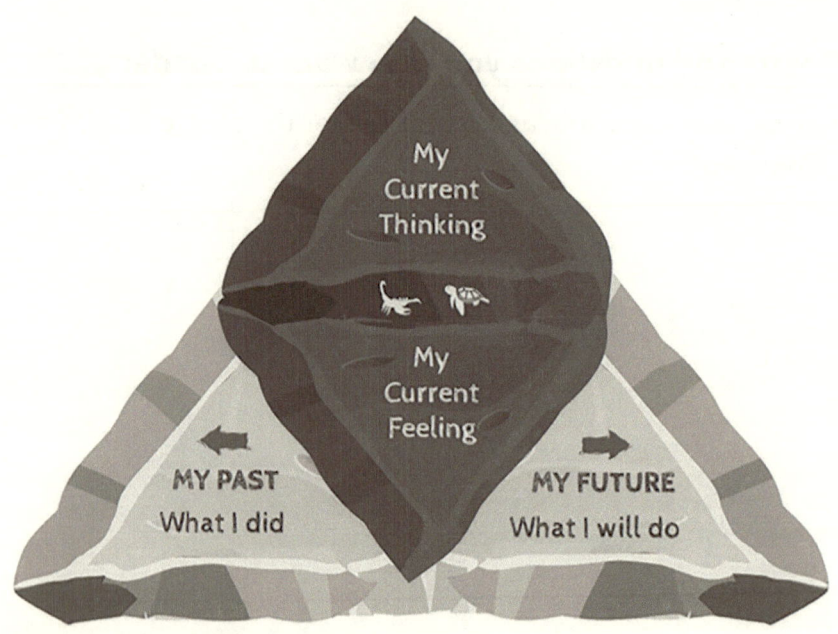

Figure 20: Life-Changing Learning Opportunities Pyramid

My Additional Current Thoughts

My Current Feelings

Actions That Will Affect My Future

CHAPTER FIFTEEN

VERY SPECIAL INDEED

Innocence Story

I recall a couple who had two boys they brought to see me four different times over two years: I saw them during their Christmas and spring breaks from school. The older brother was ten, and the younger one was eight when I first met them. Their parents always drove some thousand miles round-trip from another state for each of the four visits. During each trip, the two brothers would receive ten hours of neurofeedback whole-brain training and two and a half hours of counseling.

Their mom and dad had been happily married for fourteen years, and they both worked in the local government in their hometown. The two boys were their only children to date. When I spoke to the parents alone, they explained they were becoming increasingly concerned about their boys. They seemed to be good boys causing little trouble at home, but both had real problems at school. The older brother came to me labeled as having special needs. He was having difficulty in school with his behavior and his schoolwork. It was common for both boys to become angry and even cry when their parents asked them about how school had gone that day. The boys' parents had already met with school officials, who decided to take them out of their regular classrooms and put them in a new special needs classroom for the remainder of the school year. The boys had been in this new classroom for a few months when they came to see me for the first time.

I recall a two-hour neurofeedback brain training I had with the older boy on his second visit with me. I had just completed his two hours of brain training and I inquired, as I often do how the training was for him. I could see he had something on his mind, but he seemed to be a little hesitant to answer. I asked him, "Is there something you want to tell me?"

He said, "Yes."

I replied, "It is okay if you tell me."

What he said surprised me. He said I should not ever again show him the video that I used when he was receiving his brain training. I did not understand his response to this science video about the universe. I asked him if he could tell me why.

He looked at me with great resolve and said, "Did you hear them say the sun is going to burn up one day?"

I said, "Yes." I make it my practice to review each video before I use it to make sure it is age-appropriate, so I still did not understand what was so upsetting to him. I went on to try to use a certain type of logic, explaining to him what the video left out was it would be about five billion years before all of that would likely happen. I thought this additional information would help him feel better, knowing he had nothing to worry about because it was an exceptionally long time before this would happen. I was wrong. He quickly responded, this time with a small tear in each eye saying, "What about all the people on Earth? What will happen to them?"

That is when he touched my heart! This precious little boy with so-called special needs was thinking about people who were not even born yet and what would happen to them five billion years from now. Are you kidding me? I must say something about him. As I noted earlier, this precious little boy had a label of having special needs by his school system back home. For me, I will always remember him as exceptional and incredibly special indeed!

His younger brother came to me because he was suffering from social anxiety, not wanting to go to school, and having headaches. During my time with him in counseling, I discovered he had a history of being bullied in school, which he had never told his parents or teachers. He said he had never said anything because he did not want to get anyone in trouble. After talking with him, he was able to tell his parents.

When I saw him on one of his future visits, I was pleasantly surprised when he told me he had something he had made just for me. I asked him what it is. He reached into his book bag, pulled out a small brown bag, and gave it to me. I put my hand into the bag to find a wrapped large piece of a chocolate brownie. I said, "How did you know I liked brownies?"

He said, "You are silly. Everybody likes homemade brownies, and I made them myself last night!"

I thanked him for his thoughtful gift, and he was so right. The brownie he made for me was as good as it gets.

Some fourteen years after his last visit, I received a text from him. He said, "I just wanted you to know, Dr. Bill, I am still cooking, and here is a picture of me graduating from culinary school. Thanks for everything!" I texted him back with congratulations, and I added that even though his gift fourteen years earlier of a homemade brownie was good, I considered this text to be the best gift of all. I attached a smiley face.

Who is who?

Who had scorpion-like behaviors? _____

Who had turtle-like behaviors? _____

FOUNDATIONAL HUMAN KNOWLEDGE

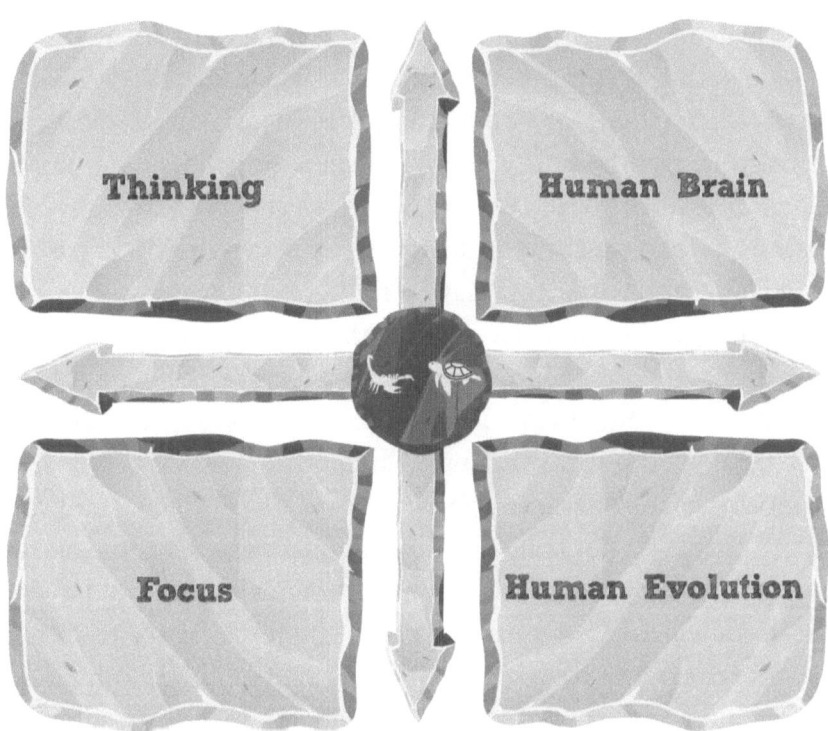

Figure 21: Chapter Fifteen - Foundational Human Knowledge

Thinking

> Thinking is a mental process used to improve one's understanding of something in an attempt to make sense of the world.

Have you been wanting a big aha moment? Wait for it. Drum roll. Thinking is composed of thoughts! Have you ever thought about where thoughts come from? I have concluded they can come from anywhere. If you are like most of us, then you know some thoughts can be way out there. I mean a wild thought like writing 28 books. Can you imagine? Okay, you think there are even wilder thoughts. You may be right.

Many people have a common thought when they enter a relationship. They believe they can change the other person to be how they want them to be, or the other person will change on their own. Now, that is a wild thought! I rarely see people just change or change because another person makes them. I am not saying people do not bend or adapt. Remember what I said about how people can act like a rubber band: when a rubber band must, it can stretch until it cannot stretch anymore. Then, once the pressure is off, the rubber band returns to how it was originally. That should explain why it looks like there is a genuine change in a person, and then over time, they go back to how they used to be. They are just doing what I call the *"human two-step"*, (dancing around and avoiding the real issues).

If a person is going to alter their thoughts, feelings, and actions significantly, they must want to change, and then they must be able to do what it takes to get there. If both conditions are not present, do not expect authentic change to occur and endure. This applies to adults only.

Children are more easily influenced and can be manipulated. Let me give you one example I sometimes see in my practice. It happens when one parent in a divorce or separation influences a child or children in some way against the other parent. This is known as parental alienation.[42] They can do this more easily with a child because human brain wiring is not complete until they are well into their 20s.[43]

Let me point out that there is much more to being an adult than just having thoughts. Having thoughts is no big deal. Most people have them. It is rather what you do with the thoughts you have that helps determine what kind of life you will have. You must learn to screen, manage, and direct your thoughts to experience life to the fullest.

Points and questions you may want to ponder:

Why do you think the little boy in the story "Innocence" who watched the video had the response he had?

Do you think most people would have thought what he did?

---

[42] https://www.ncsc.org/__data/assets/pdf_file/0014/42152/parental_alienation_Lewis.pdf.
[43] https://bigthink.com/mind-brain/adult-brain.

Human Brain

> The human brain is the part of a human being that directs the rest of the human body and is responsible for our thoughts, sensations, feelings, and actions.

You have already learned that the primary function of our brain is survival. I think it is safe to say if the human brain does not survive, then from its perspective, nothing else really matters. That is its first and foremost priority. When I talk about survival, I am talking about the human brain's main program objective to continue to exist.

As you know, that does not just involve the now but also the past and the future. It appears awareness of the past is built into the design of each human brain. This awareness of the past is not just your conscious memory but memories that go back potentially to the beginning of humankind itself. This is tied in with why we must continue to learn. Without learning, the probability of survival is diminished greatly. Have you noticed that we human beings operate cyclically? I mean we seem to have a finite number and a limited range of choices regarding how we live our lives. In my lifetime, I have seen many examples of how things operate cyclically. I have seen musical vinyl records come and go. I have seen the width of ties narrow and widen, and I have seen entire cultures fluctuate from one extreme to another and back again.

Within our essence, we are creatures of brain habits. These brain habits can be passed on from one generation to another. These brain habits emanate from the past and move into our present lives to influence our future. I know I have previously touched on some of how the human brain works. Because our brains are so important, I must go into even greater detail. Okay, this is where life becomes more interesting in relation to our brains and, thus, our very lives.

Let us talk a little about the human brain's structure and function as it relates to stress and survival during modern times.

I do not want to make this an anatomy lesson. I think it would be helpful to briefly provide you with a few theories within the last 100 years and some basic information about the anatomy of the human brain with current research concerning how our brains attempts to help each of us during times of perceived threat, change, challenge, and stress. In 1967 a neuroscientist named Paul D. MacLean brought forth the idea that all human brains function as three separate brains. MacLean called these three parts the Triune Brain. Each part was developed one before the other like a layered cake.[44]

The oldest part is the R-complex, better known as our reptilian brain. It is located at the brain stem and cerebellum, at the back of the head. The reptilian brain is about basic survival through instincts and our bodies' regulation: heartbeat, breathing, temperature control, automatic muscle movements, sleeping, and waking. The next brain layer is our limbic system, which is in the forebrain, better known by some as our paleomammalian system. It comprises the hippocampus, hypothalamus, and amygdala. This layer has a role in basic memory function, manages and improves movement, and is where emotions originate. The last and most recent brain layer is the cerebral cortex (a.k.a., cerebral mantle), and it is also known as our neomammalian brain. It comprises the outer layers of the neural tissue of our cerebrum. It is responsible for processing sensory information, communicating and understanding language, including writing

---

[44] MacLean, P. D. (1990). The triune brain in evolution: Role in paleocerebral functions. Springer Science & Business Media.

and speech, controlling voluntary movement, and handling memory, problem-solving, and planning.

In the last several years, neuroscience research has discovered:

> The Triune Brain Theory is not the best explanation of how our brain functions in everyday life or during stressful situations.

Specifically, they found emotion and cognition are not separate and distinct concerning brain function but interdependent and are always working together. There are no dedicated cognitive circuits in the brain, and the brain's cortex is much more than just the cognitive center. There are no circuits in the brain that only focus on emotion.

Some researchers today believe there is a better evolutionarily based model of how our brain functions daily and under stress. They labeled this model the adaptive brain, whose foundation is based on our brain's survival needs. Our brain uses adaptive prediction. This adaptive prediction happens because of the interdependent brain networks which use our internal and external awareness of ourselves and the world. Our brain responds to what it perceives as a threat by reducing external stress to ensure the person's survival. It does this for anything contrary to its adaptive goals: to be balanced and increase one's safety.[45]

As you now know, the human brain is more complex than most of us realize. It can do about twenty quadrillion calculations per second.[46] That is sometimes a good thing and sometimes a bad

---

[45] Steffen PR, Hedges D and Matheson R (2022) The Brain Is Adaptive Not Triune: How the Brain Responds to Threat, Challenge, and Change. Front. Psychiatry 13:802606. doi: 10.3389/fpsyt.2022.802606.

[46] Arsalidou and Taylor, 2011 M. Arsalidou, M.J. Taylor, "Is 2 + 2 = 4?: Meta-analyses of brain areas needed for numbers and calculations" Neuroimage, 54 (2011), pp. 2382-2393.

thing. It is good because 95 percent of what it takes to operate as a human being is done very quickly for us beyond our conscious awareness.[47] This can also be bad for us sometimes because of our brain's desire for speed and efficiency.

Occasionally, if our brain does not know what to do, it will guess. Due to how sensory information is received, the executive, conscious part of our brain is always the last to know what is going on. It means that actions are often taken before the executive center of your brain gives much input. That can be problematic because the executive center of our brain, which is a part of our cerebral cortex, is there to consider the alternatives, and this often involves looking at the big picture. You may know this better as having a perspective.

There is good news. The good news is that if you want to be more consciously involved in living and making decisions for your life, you will want to develop your brain's executive center. There are a number of ways to do this. I suggest you start by slowing down and not making decisions quickly, taking some time before acting on things, and saying no to your instincts sometimes, particularly to your instincts governing fight, flight, freeze, or fornication.[48] These are the four big ones I see most often, giving people the most trouble and life distress across most ages in my private practice. I did not say it is easy to say no to your instincts, but it can be done. And, no, you do not have to live by yourself in a cave or on a deserted island to do it.

You can tell if this is something you want to explore if your life seems to be out of control and you cannot find the solutions to your life problems, no matter how hard you try. This is a clear

---

[47] Szegedy-Maszak M. Mysteries of the mind. US News World Rep. 2005 Feb 28;138(7):52-4, 57-8, 60-1. PMID: 15765847.
[48] Adcock, P. (2015). Master Your Brain: Training Your Mind for Success in Life. Sterling.

sign you are most likely operating on autopilot and need to find ways to increase your insight. If you choose to seek the right kind of help, life can improve for sure.

Points and questions you may want to ponder:

In the story "Innocence," how well do you think certain parts of the brain of the little boy who watched the video were working?

Would you have concluded what he did about the sun and the people on Earth?

Focus

> Focus is the process by which people eliminate extraneous variables to take possible actions because of their interests and perceived importance.

There is a great deal of activity going on in the world around us at any given time. It is by focusing that we can pay attention to what is important to each of us as an individual. Without focus, we are left at the mercy of whatever comes our way. **A lack of focus is often partially responsible for a *life not well-lived*.** I have heard some people say, "Focus does not matter." They say, "Just go with the flow. Take whatever comes your way. One brown-haired man is just as good as another." I would suggest you not listen to them if you are interested in being a winner in life.

To be a winner, you must approach life deliberately. By winning, I mean you have the best life possible given the context within which you live. This implies that you must not waste valuable resources but channel your efforts into what will produce the greatest rewards.

Focus can be both internal and external.[49] Internal focus is about being aware of your state of being, which involves knowing your strengths and weaknesses and how you are using them. It is like employing a device to ascertain the level of your body's temperature. External focus pays attention to the context of your surroundings. It is focused on what is going on around you in the world. It is the combination and balance of these two types of focus that allow human beings to survive and even thrive.

---

[49] fastcompany.com/3036293/the-difference-between-internal-and-external-focus-and-why-it-matters.

Internal focus matters because if you do not know what you want in life, you are not likely to find it. External focus matters because if you do not open your eyes to see both the big picture as well as the details of life, you will miss much of what positives it has in store for you.

In my private practice, I help people who are in bondage because they either have learned how to focus wrongly or decided to shut their eyes completely to protect themselves from disappointment and pain. As a result, they are left to stumble through life and complain about how bad life is for them. In their minds, they have become victims. But really, it is due to the lack of correct focus at the right time.

I am in no way minimizing their pain; I am confident their pain is real. I am only letting you know there is a way to have a happier and more gratifying life than only accepting being a victim. Once we have been victimized for whatever reason, what was done is done. You cannot change that fact, but you can change your mindset. For this very reason, we can change our focus, let go of the negative past, and begin to move on with our lives in search of a better future. If one chooses to retain a negative focus, one will likely experience more of life's negatives. If one decides to focus on the positives of life, so one will experience more of what is positive, too. That is just how it works. It is not instantaneous, but what you focus on will dictate where you are destined to arrive and reside.

Allow me to give you another example of what I mean. Let us take driving a vehicle as an example. I have been driving for almost half a century. I have noticed that when driving, once I turn my head in a particular direction while holding the steering wheel, the vehicle will head in the direction I am focusing on. As it is with automobiles, so it is in life. What you focus on is where you will live and how you will feel about it. If you *focus* on what is *wrong* in your life, you will *feel* what is *wrong* in your life, then you will experience much pain in your life, and thus, your life will not be filled with peace, joy, or happiness. I am not saying ignore what is wrong with life but rather don't only focus on it without doing something about it, so that you can spend more time enjoying what life you do have.

Points and questions you may want to ponder:

Do you think the little boy who watched the video in the "Innocence" story was focused on more than himself?

Human Evolution

> Human evolution is the biological connection human beings have to past generations, designed to help the species improve and adjust better to their current environment and continue to survive.

In this self-improvement book, I will try to avoid the divide that exists between those who spend their time with what is true or false concerning how we got here or how long we have been here. Instead, I will speak to what is happening now regarding humankind and evolution. From what I can gather, there appears to be more agreement regarding the role of evolution regarding other life forms on this planet than it does when it comes to human beings. I am interested in human evolution from the perspective of how it influences change in all of us. If, as life forms, we are indeed influenced by evolution in the way it appears other forms of life are, then it seems to me we can benefit from a better understanding of the process. I am not an expert in evolution, but I do have my thoughts and observations that I appreciate the opportunity to share with you.

I hope we can agree that evolution involves time and human beings' experiences interacting with their environment for change to take place. Additionally, as life forms, human beings are designed to survive, if possible. Okay, with these things in mind, now what? As you may remember, science agrees that our interaction with the environment can change our genetic makeup, and we pass this genetic information to the next generation.[50] Wow, are you starting to get the picture? **You and I are faced with what is happening in real-time around us and pre-configured in ways that provide a unique**

---

[50] **Natural Selection Reduced Diversity on Human Y Chromosomes** Wilson Sayres MA, Lohmueller KE, Nielsen R (2014) Natural Selection Reduced Diversity on Human Y Chromosomes. PLOS Genetics 10(1): e1004064.

range of possibilities for our thoughts, feelings, and actions as part of our evolution and thus our future survival.

I believe there is a delicate balance to all of this, which will surely work for the betterment of humankind and this planet if maintained in the correct ways. I can hear you saying, *I can go along with this to some point, so what is the problem?* I am so glad you asked. I see the root cause of some of humanity's problems coming from the process of evolution and its connection to current technology. Allow me to explain further. It can be argued that humanity not only wants technology but is now obsessed with it. I believe we have gone way past the want, and we are now in the need stage for technology. How many people do you know would choose to remove all technology from modern warfare worldwide?

So, what is the problem, you may be asking yourself, concerning the change of humankind from wanting technology to needing (being dependent on) technology?

Currently, technology is like an addictive drug for many. Like an addictive drug, the more you get, the more you want, and ultimately, you go from want to needing in a never-ending attempt to survive. We appear to be caught in a vicious cycle because of our need to survive and our relationship with technology. Since our survival instinct is our strongest instinct, we find ourselves constantly looking for answers to our insecurities. The problem is we have attached our very survival to technology. Hence, the more we advance in technology, the more insecure we become, and the more we must have new technology to help us feel more secure. This is an addictive cycle that, in the end, never has a happy ending. It can be said that, technology is moving faster than we are evolving. It is like having your eyes exposed to extremely bright light right after you come out of the dark, in contrast to having your eyes gradually introduced to bright light over an extended time frame. Which of these do you think would be more painful and less helpful? Yep, you got it! It is not just what but how that matters in our lives.

As I imagine you do, I look around myself and see so many people lost and confused about how to navigate life. We are living in a time when anything goes because many people now feel, *What does it matter anyway?* I am concerned that many people have lost the connection to each other and our planet. This is dangerous to us all because it affects not only an individual's now, but all of our evolutionary futures. I am not here to judge or condemn you or anyone else for life choices. I am only trying to raise your awareness and share my knowledge to increase your understanding, This is how you acquire the foundational human knowledge you need to survive our troubling times. This type of knowledge can be used to create positive change in this world if you choose to use it constructively.

Points and questions you may want to ponder:

In the story "Innocence", how was human evolution illustrated?

Why do you think what would happen to human beings in the future mattered to the little boy?

Do you think most people you know would care about what will happen to humanity five billion years from now?

Life-Changing Learning Opportunities

Please pause for a moment and list some of your thoughts and feelings from what you have just experienced. After doing this, I recommend you write down the actions you will take to affect your future for the better. Do this based on what comes first to your mind after reading the story with its accompanying foundational human knowledge.

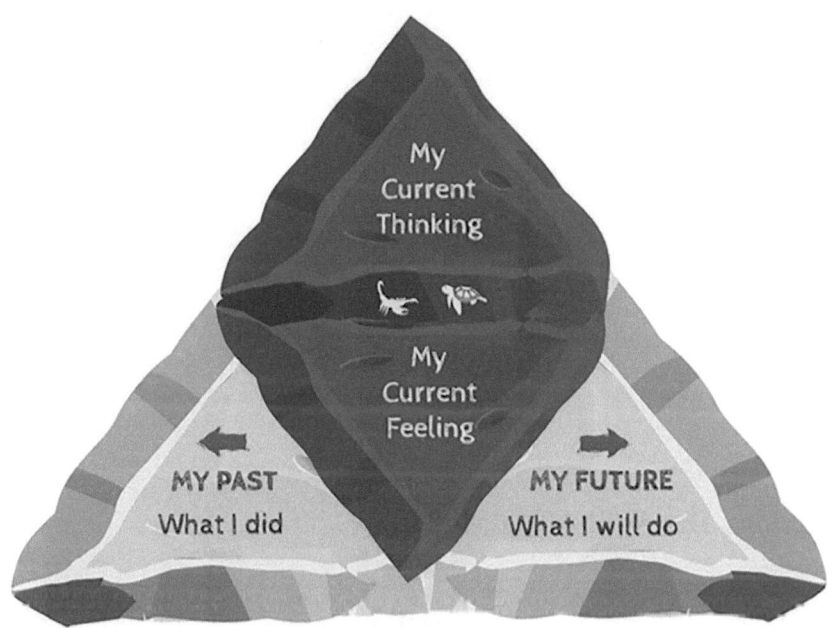

Figure 22: Life-Changing Learning Opportunities Pyramid

My Additional Current Thoughts

My Current Feelings

Actions That Will Affect My Future

CHAPTER SIXTEEN

FINDING YOUR WAY

Being Authentic Story

I received a call from a man named Bobby who wanted to come and visit me to discuss some challenges he was having regarding his life direction. At our first two-hour meeting together, he began by telling me about his accomplished family members: his father, an accountant; his mother, a pharmacist; his older sister, a medical doctor; and his brother, an attorney. He described his brother as Mr. Perfect, who could do no wrong, and his sister, who was all about *"the money."* He stated his parents were only *into their work*. He felt there was a lot of pressure on him to become a doctor to be valued and finally become somebody to his parents. He said, "In my family, only performance matters." It became clear to me that he had been on a rather long and painful journey.

This young man spent the next two hours explaining how he had worked hard in high school to get into a good college, then proceeded to medical school, completed two years of study before hitting a wall, which he could not find a way over, around, or under, no matter what he did. After completing his second year of medical school, he switched to dental school and completed one year when he hit another wall. That is where he was when he decided to reach out for help for the very first time in his life.

He continued after a short break to provide me with some history of his teenage drug use. He explained he began taking over-the-counter medications as non-prescribed drugs and smoking marijuana shortly after he turned fourteen. He said, "I used drugs because it was my only way of escaping from all of life's pressures."

He went on to talk about how fake social media was. He did not understand why people his age would need to have twenty thousand so-called friends and post everything about their lives online, especially given that most of it was made up anyway.

He was not happy about many of his school experiences. For instance, he spoke of graduate school and some experiences he had in study groups. He told me it was common for him to be in a study group where he had to do most of the other people's work because they just wanted to get by with the minimum. Others in his classes wanted to borrow his notes because he often set the curve. He felt used. He was somewhat discouraged about his fellow students. He gave several examples of how he was aware of those he thought were good friends, only to find out later they had been unfaithful to their current boyfriends or girlfriends. He said almost everyone he knew was doing it!

He stopped for a moment, looked at me, and said, "What is wrong with me?"

I replied, "Wrong with you?"

He said, "I do not trust people. They just think of themselves." Throughout the rest of the session, I continued to do my best by addressing all his questions.

I told him he was not alone and that there are many others seeking answers to why people are the way they are. One day, I might even write a book to offer my thoughts on these and other important topics. He encouraged me to do so, and we ended his first visit to my office.

I continued to see him another four or five times while he was still in town, and I spoke to him by phone a few more times over the next three months. I do not know if he finally completed dental school. I choose to think that no matter what career and life path he has undertaken, he will find a way to be happy in life.

Who is who?

Who had scorpion-like behaviors? _____

Who had turtle-like behaviors? _____

FOUNDATIONAL HUMAN KNOWLEDGE

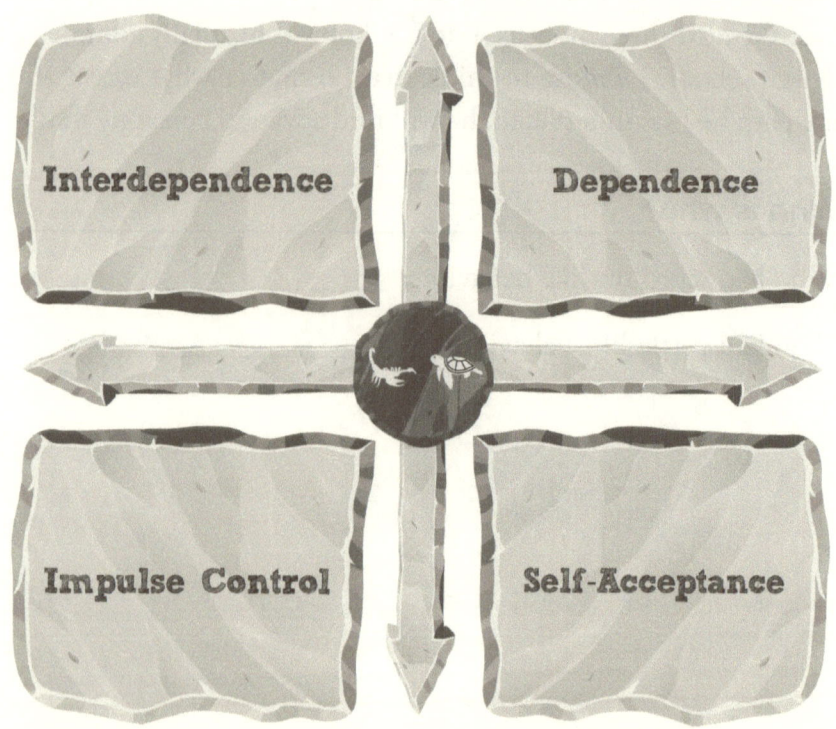

Figure 23: Chapter Sixteen- Foundational Human Knowledge

Interdependence

> Interdependence is a state of being that involves being connected with something. The well-being of each depends on this connection to function well.

When I think of interdependence, the first thing that comes to my mind involves my human anatomy. You may have noticed most of us are born with two eyes, two ears, two hands, and two arms. I think you are beginning to get my point; there is more than one, and they must work together in harmony for us to function optimally.

From my experience, I know that when I need to unload my car, it is much better when I carry things with both hands instead of one. I also noticed when I ride a bike, it is so much easier to go faster and further with less energy when pedaling with two legs working together as opposed to just one. Since the parts of our body are interdependent, I do not think it is much of a stretch to conclude it works this way outside our body.

I also know this from personal experience: if I want to pick up something like a canoe and have a friend who can pick up the front part while I pick up the back, it is much easier to move if we work together. Over the years, humankind has learned a lot about how our entire planet is connected. You can see how interconnected we are regarding our need for food, clothing, healthcare, protection, water, energy, and shelter, to name only a few examples. I am sure you can think of many ways you are interdependent with others.

I mentioned earlier that I am an only child. I did not share that I do not always like playing with others! Sometimes, you may feel that way, too. During my lifetime, this world has continued to become more complex and difficult to understand.

If I understand anything, it is that our interdependence was designed to be a benefit for all of us. For that to occur, some people must stop using it to take advantage of others before we reach a point of no return. It is the very fact that our interdependence exists that must cause us to pause and consider the future of our planet and our survival. **We will never learn how to maximize our interdependence if we continue to look for it from a place of singularity, seen only through the eyes of one or two super-powerful nations. Instead, we need to develop and maximize our interdependence further through multipolarity.** We must seek the answers we require from a place that includes all by giving everyone access and a platform to amplify their voices so that they can be heard. With people having an opportunity for equal access and participation in their societies and on the world stage, the people of the world will finally be able to contribute fully and gain all the benefits of interdependence, and each of us will win!

Points and questions you may want to ponder:

How was interdependence highlighted in the story "Being Authentic"?

How well did interdependence work for Bobby?

Dependence

> Dependence is an absolute connection of a person to another person, group, government, place, or thing for perceived survival.

People can develop a level of dependence on about anything. It can be drugs, alcohol, money, fame, work, lifestyle, power, and control to name just a few.

I work with a lot of couples, and dependence is a topic that comes up frequently. I see many people in relationships in which one person has more power and thus has potential control in many ways over the other person. This creates an imbalance. I have discovered that power imbalances in relationships are not always helpful and can be harmful. Having greater power can tempt one member of the relationship to take advantage of the other, leading to a loss of respect for both people toward one another.

I recall a couple I worked with several years ago; they decided the husband would quit his job, put his career on hold, and stay home to care for their newborn while the wife would go back to work. The man was not making as much money as his wife had before the child was born, so this seemed to make the best financial sense. Over time, as the child grew older, the man became overdependent on his wife for everything in finance. He even had to ask her for lunch money. For him, this was painful, and he felt demeaned and emasculated. As his wife became more successful at her job, her independence grew. She worked long hours, meeting the demands of her employer. The couple was slowly growing apart, even though they lived in the same house. They each had roles to play but lost their connection to one another. When they were on the verge of divorce, they sought professional help from me.

It is a common experience for couples to see me after one or both have left the relationship psychologically or emotionally. I am happy to say this couple finally re-established a genuine connection to one another after I had some sessions with each of them. They found a way to make the necessary adjustments by changing the imbalance in their dependence on one another, which reduced their power and control challenges.

This promptly helped them to regain the mutual respect they had lost for each other before they came to see me. I would like to say this positive outcome always happens when a couple sees me because of dependency challenges, but I cannot. **There is a real danger when interdependence changes to dependence by one participant in a relationship.** It might work for a while, but it can also divide a relationship to the point of dissolving it.

Points and questions you may want to ponder:

Was dependence a good or a bad thing for Bobby in the story from his point of view?

Impulse Control

> Impulse control is the act of decreasing one's automatic responses to the environment by increasing the activation of the human brain's executive center. It allows for more logical deliberation and action.

All humans have impulses. Impulse control mastery is vital if you want the best possible life. When humans do not control their impulses, they can be very destructive to themselves and the rest of the world. Thus human beings are in a constant battle, which takes place in their minds. This is one of the reasons society seeks to socialize each of us because they cannot risk leaving us to our impulses.

We are born wanting what we want, and we die wanting what we want. We all, therefore, have impulses that want to control how we think, feel, and act. It is part of being a human being. I cannot recall any other time in history when more people have been able to get what they want so quickly. This is better known as instant gratification. When one gets their wants satisfied almost immediately, there is less need for impulse control. You only require impulse control when you do not get what you want. **The more we get what we want, the more likely we will have less control over our impulses which can eventually lead to little or no impulse control.** This is because of how our brains are wired.

You already know that as thought is reinforced by action, it will become more likely that we will follow through with the same action again. It gets easier over time, requiring less and less effort to do so. This is why we must learn how to control our impulses better to be successful in life.

You can observe the desire for instant gratification in children who are two years old or thereabouts. This stage is known as "the terrible twos"[51] by many parents because this period in a child's development is all about "Me," "I want," "Mine," "More," and "Why?" At this age and stage of development, children can be sweet one minute and terrors the next. Often, dissatisfaction on the child's part is openly demonstrated when they do not get their way, regardless of their environment. This can be no fun for anyone around them, particularly if you find yourself in an airplane a few seats away on a three-hour flight while a child is being taught how to control their impulses. Has this ever happened to you?

It is helpful to remind oneself that this is a normal part of growing up, and it aids in making us become healthy human beings. If we do not learn to control our impulses early in our lives, real problems can develop. When we do not keep our impulses in control and there is little conscious thought involved before acting, there can be significant consequences for both children and adults.

Different parts of our brain are either engaged or not when it comes to impulse control. As stated earlier in this book, the prefrontal cortex plays a major role in controlling impulses in healthy human beings.

As I walk among people, I only need to observe their behavior to see which part of their brain is running the show. Based on how the parts of our brains come online involving our instincts, emotions, and rational thought, we each must do all we can to strengthen the impulse center of our brain. Likewise, it is equally important not to use substances that weaken these same centers of the brain. If you want to develop strong impulse control, you must begin to think of others as well as your desires. Poor impulse control is linked to being selfish.

---

[51] https://www.healthline.com/health/parenting/terrible-twos.

You can perhaps now see why we have more people today with little or no impulse control than at any previous time in recent history. All you must do is look around and open your eyes and ears to see and hear all the messages from those trying to sell you something or tell you how you should think, feel, and what action you should take. The messages come in the form of something like this: "Do what you want when you want it because you deserve it, so buy their product or use their service!" Considering others is not part of these messages.

I am in favor of being self-centered, which is different than being selfish. After all, if you do not take action in your best interest, who would you expect to do it for you?

That said, I would ask you to consider every action you take before taking it and choose those that will not hurt you, others, or this planet. *Great*, you may say, *What does that leave?* Those actions which are win-win.

The world is in real trouble, and if humanity is going to prevail, it must find a way to strengthen and master its impulses. We have become accustomed to living in a society where many are making large sums of money off people who have less and less impulse control, and some have even developed what is known in my field as a mental illness—*Impulse Control* Disorder. This is a condition in which a person has reached a threshold of having real trouble *controlling* their emotions or behaviors, which can lead to major consequences. Often, their behaviors violate the rights of others or conflict with societal norms and the law.[52] I believe this is a severe problem worldwide and can no longer be condoned or ignored. It must be addressed with the utmost urgency.

---

[52] Impulse Control Disorder & Addiction: Causes, Symptoms & Treatment. (2023, March 22). American Addiction Centers. https://americanaddictioncenters.org/co-occurring-disorders/impulse-control-disorder.

Points and questions you may want to ponder:

Was impulse control a factor in the story "Being Authentic"?

Do you think Bobby's early drug use affected him long-term?

Self-Acceptance

> Self-acceptance is being at peace with who you perceive yourself to be.

Self-acceptance is best achieved if it is not based on one's performance. As you know, one's performance often varies, but I do not believe self-acceptance has to. I have found it is possible to have self-acceptance throughout your life.

To be human is, without a doubt, a challenge of the highest order. It often comes down to what to accept and what not to accept, and how each option affects us in the end. There is a great deal of struggle and pain connected to this challenge. You already know we were designed to want what we want, but do you know we're also designed not to always get what we want. I have realized that even when one gets what they want, it is not always what is best for them.

As you know many human beings are regularly assaulted from all sides by media of all kinds as to how they should look, what products or services they should buy and use, and ultimately who they are as a person. We live in a world ruled by special interest groups, which by their very nature, seek to manipulate each of us in almost every area of our lives.

This goes on right from the beginning of life and is relentless until we exhale our last breath. Sometimes, it is done very subtly and deceptively. In other cases, it may be well-intended, but it is still manipulative. You may have noticed people out in the world that think they know what is best for each of us. I find it particularly interesting is when people who want me to do what they say is right often have something to either lose or to gain from my behavior. When I look at different situations, I try to pause and see what is in it for the other person before choosing a course of action.

I have pointed out in this book already that there is only one you. I believe it was intended that way for a purpose. The purpose is for you to become your best you. To do this, self-acceptance is required. Please note: you must first learn to accept yourself before you can truly accept others. It is difficult to achieve this if you do not know who you are. There are those out there who can help you, but ultimately, this is your job. By the way, if you spend all your time listening to the world's hype by seeking to escape reality, you will likely be lost much of your life and may never find who you were designed to be.

Many of the problems I see in people result from a lack of self-acceptance, in which they tend to blame others for how they think and feel about themselves. You must learn that you are not here to control others, nor do you want to. As human beings, we can only work on controlling ourselves. For many, self-acceptance will help them to let go of unnecessary pain that comes with trying to control others. It is through accepting yourself that you can become healed and whole; this is absolute freedom. If you need help with self-acceptance, please reach out to a licensed behavioral health professional who has expertise and experience in the areas you will need help with.

Points and questions you may want to ponder:

Do you think Bobby in the story "Being Authentic" was able to find self-acceptance?

Life-Changing Learning Opportunities

Please pause for a moment and list some of your thoughts and feelings from what you have just experienced. After doing this, I recommend you write down the actions you will take to affect your future for the better. Do this based on what comes first to your mind after reading the story with its accompanying foundational human knowledge.

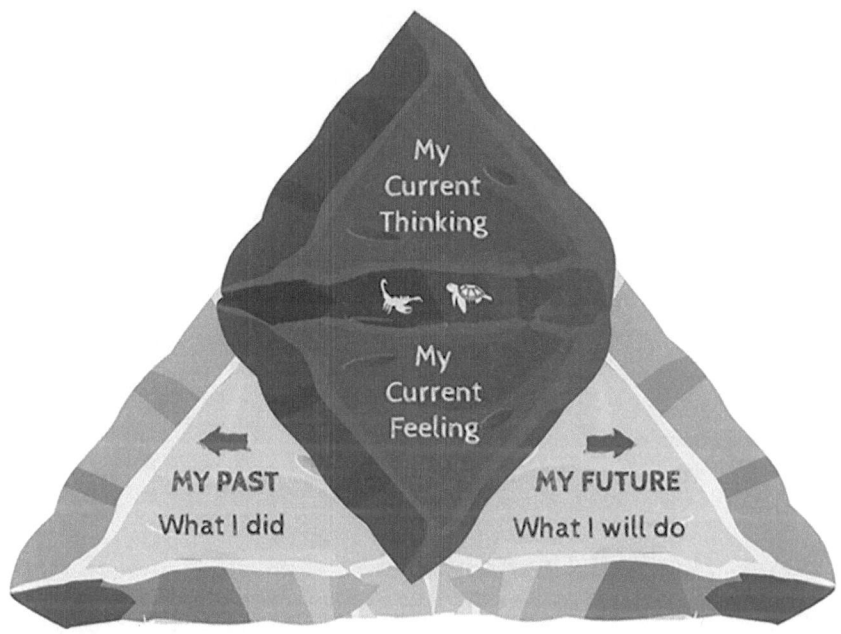

Figure 24: Life-Changing Learning Opportunities Pyramid

My Additional Current Thoughts

My Current Feelings

Actions That Will Affect My Future

CHAPTER SEVENTEEN

WELCOME TO THE REAL WORLD

It Is Just Business Story

Early in my career, I was introduced to the unique world of big business. This happened in a town not far from where I grew up. In it was a large company connected to the automobile industry. I had always liked cars and trucks since I was a little boy. It seemed reasonable to me to go and explore the possibilities of employment with this company.

One day, I mustered the courage to go to the company's main office building. I had just walked in when I noticed a woman behind a long counter. I introduced myself to her as someone interested in employment with the company. She seemed to be somewhat surprised and caught off guard.

After a few moments she told me this was not the human resource building, and as she began to give me the address, I heard a voice behind me saying, "So you're looking for a job?" I quickly turned and saw a rather large man whom I estimated was in his mid-sixties. He was dressed in a casual long-sleeve shirt, blue jeans, and tennis shoes. He apparently had asked me the question.

I said, "Yes sir, I am."

He said, "If you have a moment, I want to talk to you in my office." I said, "Sure" and followed him down a long hall to an office. He opened the door, and we entered. It was a large space which seemed like the size of a small house.

He asked me to take a seat and he sat in front of me in an oversized chair behind his large desk. He cleared his throat and asked, "So, why do you want to work here, and what can you do for us?" I calmly answered, "I live close by, and I have been aware of your company for years. I know you are the best at what you make, and I want to work for the best."

He laughed a belly laugh and asked in a low tone this time, "So, what can you do for us?"

Without hesitation, I said, "Whatever you need me to do. I am not afraid of hard work."

"Okay," he said, "How much do you expect as payment?"

I said, "Sir, you pay me what you think I am worth, and that will work for me."

He belly laughed again. He then stood up, paused to write something on a piece of paper that he gave to me, and said, "Okay, come back next Monday and be ready to work."

I shook his hand and thanked him, and he escorted me to the nearest exit.

As I walked to my car after this unusual encounter, I had no idea what I was being hired for or what I would receive as my payment. I was so excited that I had a job waiting for me, and I would start in a few days, having just met a nice man. I later found out the man I had met was the vice president of the whole company and one of the original two founders. He was held in high regard by all the members of the company.

That weekend seemed to go by fast and, before I knew it, it was Monday morning. I had no idea what to wear because I completely forgot to ask in my moment of excitement, so I decided it would be safe to wear dress shoes, slacks, and a dress shirt with a tie. When I arrived at the address I was given on the piece of paper, I walked to the door, opened it, and walked in like I owned the place. Before me was the kind man I had met the previous Friday afternoon.

"He said, I am glad to see you. Are you ready to work?"

I replied, "Yes, Sir!" He took me to a separate area of the building and introduced me to a team leader. "Here is Bill, he is going to need a desk and a chair. This is his first day."

The team leader shook my hand, looked over to the vice president, and said, "I will take good care of him."

The team leader then took me to another part of the building, where the sales team was located. They were divided into six teams of four people who had a desk with a phone and a computer readout with phone numbers and company names. I was directed to my desk and told to familiarize myself with what the company sold and start calling the phone numbers. I could watch and hear other sales members talking on the phone, and before long, I added my voice to the group.

Fast forward three weeks, and I came to work as usual, but this time, I was told to go directly to the vice president's office. I did as I was instructed. His door was open, and when he saw me, he said, "Bill, how is it going?"

I replied, "I am learning a lot each day, and I think I am getting the hang of it."

He said, "Great. I wanted to see you today to offer you a unique opportunity to go on the road."

In my short time with the company, I had become aware that there was one individual who would come to the office about once a month—he was the only one for over six years who was "on the road." I responded to the vice president with "On the road?"

He explained there was a need to expand the company's territory. He wanted me to show the company's products across four additional new states. I would have a work partner who would work the phone and schedule my daily visits to show the company's products.

I said, "If that is what you need, count me in."

I went home that night thinking life had just become more interesting. I did not mind the phone work, but this new opportunity would allow me to go to parts of the United States I had never been to and stretch my legs.

The next day, I headed out to showcase our products. We had great products, so it seemed wherever I went, city after city, people were interested, and I was successful. After being on the road for about three months, I visited another new dealership and showed our products. The buyer was not in, but the general manager I spoke to was excited and told me he would talk to the buyer and get back to me.

I said, "Great." I was due to return for a week at the home office, so I told him I would follow up with him by phone in a day or two, and I left to catch a plane back home.

On the second day back at my office, I called the person I had met to see what kind of order his buyer wanted to place. He told me he had talked to the buyer, but before committing to an order, the buyer wanted to speak to their company's owner, a Mr. K., who lived in another state.

I said, "Perfect. I will give you a few more days before I call you back."

He agreed.

The next day I was at the office when I heard over the sales team's intercom that Team B had just taken the single largest order in the company's fifteen-year history. Everyone was so excited that they spontaneously started clapping. As part of my excitement and joy for Team B, I went to their team leader to congratulate him myself. He said he did nothing but accept a call from the owner of a large multi-state network of dealerships, who had called from a state Team B covered, and he took the large order. I asked him the name of the owner and immediately realized what had happened. The order had come from the dealership's owner, whom I had shown the products to and had been waiting to hear from.

After thinking about it for a few moments, I went to the nearest phone and called my dealer contact, and he answered. He immediately recognized my voice and was excited to tell me he had talked to his buyer. The buyer told him that the owner had placed the order from where he lived. After some small talk, I hung up. I had confirmed what I thought. This is where I learned more about life than I had expected or even wanted.

I said to myself, "I just need to talk to my company's president, and he will do what is right when he knows the whole truth. He will give credit where credit is due, including appropriate financial rewards. You know: do the right thing, be fair." With those thoughts, I went to the president, who was now running the sales team directly since the vice president had retired. I told him the truth, and he said he would take care of it. I thought it a short meeting.

An hour after I met with him, I was escorted to the door, and my employment was terminated. Two weeks later, I received my last check, which did not include a commission for the largest order the company had ever received. That was given to the other team instead. I was sad they did not choose to do the right thing.

Who is who?

Who had scorpion-like behaviors? _____

Who had turtle-like behaviors?_____

FOUNDATIONAL HUMAN KNOWLEDGE

Figure 25: Chapter Seventeen - Foundational Human Knowledge

Talent

> Talent is a unique ability or abilities inherent in each of us from birth to be used to help us be naturally successful at some things without being taught.

I want you to think about what your talents are. Remember, it is something you can do that comes naturally to you. It may be that you are good at sports, have a great singing voice, are highly intelligent, or excel at something else. **Having a special talent requires you to be special from the outset. If you have at least one talent, then you must be special. Whatever talents you have are part of what makes you unique and special.**

The population throughout the world today is about 8 billion people give or take a few.[53] Are you aware that from the beginning of humankind, approximately 80 billion people have been born? About ten percent are still alive today, and you are one of them!

Can we agree that there has never been an exact you? There is currently not another exact you, and I think it is safe to say it is highly unlikely there will ever be another exact you in the future. If you accept these statements to be true, then you are a one-of-one. That makes you incredibly special and rare, indeed.

I want to share a unique experience I had years ago when I worked in South Florida. In my line of work, I meet all kinds of people from all over the world. I remember someone whom I only saw once for a two-hour session. At the end of our time together, he requested that I walk with him to his car because he wanted to show me something.

---

[53] worldometers.info/world-population/.

His car was parked right in front of where we met, and I was done for the day, so I agreed to go with him. We went to his car, and he opened the trunk. He reached in and pulled out a rather unusual bag made of fine leather with a special seal on it. I had never seen a bag quite like it in my whole life. He put the bag in my left hand and said, "What you are now holding is $250 million U.S. dollars in rare uncut gemstones." He then asked me to reach into the trunk and pull out another bag. I did as he requested. He said, "You are now holding in your right hand a bag of fine jewels worth another $250 million." At that point, I found myself holding in my left and right hands the equivalent of $500 million dollars. It was, as you can imagine, a unique experience.

We exchanged some small talk, and I put the bags back in his car trunk. He then said, "The reason I wanted to share this with you is that I wanted you to understand that how you helped me today was worth more to me than what you held in your hands. I just wanted to say thank you in my own way by giving you something unique in return!"

I assured him he had done so. We said our goodbyes and got into our cars. I never heard from him again. I can only tell you he had all the money he could spend but was unhappy because he was not using his natural talents.

Working in my profession, I have realized many people all over this world do the same thing, turning a blind eye to their true self in pursuit of power and fame gained from making as much money as they can as fast as they can. If you are unhappy despite all you possess (this could be your power, position, reputation, and so on in life), you may want to take a closer look inward and seek to find and hear that small, soft voice you have been trying to ignore inside you for some time now. No matter what some people say, you really can have it all!

Points and questions you may want to ponder:

Why was talent important in the story "It Is Just Business"?

Do you think talent mattered to the vice president of the company who hired me?

Leadership

> Leadership is a position one holds and actions one takes that involve power and influence over people.

When I worked in the corporate world, the most challenging part of my job dealt with the so-called leaders. They were, by their title, *leaders*, but many of them had no idea what true leadership was about and how to lead. People followed them only because they had to, or they would have work consequences, such as losing their job due to something their boss did not like.

You may have noticed scorpion-like people rise to the top in many organizations and companies until something happens, and they cannot go any further. Then they will move on and start all over again, and this cycle will go on and on until they age out. They can do this because, in many businesses worldwide, scorpion-like leaders are in high demand. This is due to some business owners who have adopted a business model that encourages their employees to do whatever it takes to make as much profit as possible. Many leaders have accepted this business practice and think of it as "Just good business." This form of leadership and business practice is oppressive and very short-sighted. In my experience, the best form of leadership is when one looks to improve all who are involved and not only the business.

The objective of many big businesses of a few big winners and everyone else loses is no longer sustainable. This is partly why the world seems to be on the decline like never before. **Leaders all over this world must wake up soon and change how they treat their employees and customers if all of us are going to have a chance to experience a better future.** My final thought for now on leadership, is that leaders are both born and made.

I have found you cannot be a true leader until you first learn how to follow. This is when you will understand that true leadership is not about power, control, or position but about being a servant to others.

One of the most rewarding moments in my career to date was when I had the opportunity as a healthcare leader to represent a group of hard-working, committed healthcare workers who had accomplished something extraordinary together. Over eight years, they had discovered a way to stop the transmission of HIV from nearly five hundred confirmed HIV-positive mothers to their newborn babies. This was due to a specific program design and consistent deployment. This accomplishment occurred while the rest of the world had an average of a 25 percent transmission rate from HIV-positive mothers to their newborns. Even though this took place some time ago, I remember it clearly.

I got on a plane in Orlando and flew to where The Joint Commission was having its national convention in Chicago. At that time, The Joint Commission was the largest and most prestigious healthcare accrediting body in the world. After arriving and getting myself ready, it was time to accept the prestigious national award on behalf of all the ten-thousand-plus employees of the mega healthcare system in which I was employed. I took a big breath, moved to the podium, and spoke to the executive hospital leaders and The Joint Commission representatives present from all over the United States of America. In front of this group of top executives in healthcare, I accepted the Ernest Amory Codman Award.[54] This National

---

[54] Soza-Vento, R. M., Flowers, L., Munroe, A. E., Fritz, K., Rua-Dobles, A., Munroe, C., & Singer, B. (2007). Reducing Perinatal HIV Transmission Among HIV–Infected Pregnant Women. The Joint Commission Journal on Quality and Patient Safety, 33(4), 187–192. https://doi.org/10.1016/s1553-7250(07)33021-3.

Health Care Award for Performance Measurement Process in the hospital category was awarded to just one hospital that year. After accepting the award as a servant leader on behalf of this incredible group of healthcare professionals, I spoke briefly and reminded the audience: "There can be no healthcare if we do not take care of the healthcare workers who give much of their lives serving others."

Today, I believe this recognition for healthcare workers is needed more than ever.

Points and questions you may want to ponder:

How was leadership portrayed in the story "It is Just Business"?

What type of leader do you prefer?

Conflict

> Conflict is the natural and inevitable discord that occurs between unique human beings and within one's self.

I find many people try to avoid conflict. They seek to avoid it because to engage in it causes a change in their emotional state from positive or neutral to negative. Given there are so many differences among people, we must learn how to manage conflict. Do you know some people thrive on conflict and seek it? You may be one of them or know of someone who is.

These people may be uncomfortable if there is not a certain level of conflict in their lives. They will even create levels of conflict if it does not occur naturally. Living in conflict can become addictive, and it is a form of life energy for those who need it to feel they are alive. It becomes something like a drug that is used to self-medicate.

If you are naturally an avoider of conflict and try to avoid it at all costs, then you have some work to do. I say this because it appears conflict is not just inevitable but a major part of our everyday life in our world today. I do not see this fact changing anytime soon. It will benefit you and those you love to get particularly good at managing it. Right now, I can hear you saying to yourself, "So, how do I do that?" My answer to you is straightforward, but it is not always easy.

The best way to deal with conflict is not to take it personally all the time. When someone disagrees with you, that is not necessarily an attack on you. You are more than your thoughts, feelings, and actions. You can remind yourself that your human value is not based on people agreeing with you. You do not have to try to get your self-esteem from others. Sometimes, life will push you into conflict with others. It helps if you try your best to remain in a neutral or positive place.

Since all of us are unique in many ways, it is not surprising that we do not think alike or always see things the same way. We must make room for our differences. All the time, I see people who are hurt emotionally because of such things. Have you ever heard about the concept of agreeing to disagree? What that means is one can disagree, and this is okay sometimes. I propose we continue to challenge one another by exploring our different points of view, taking the best of them, and employing them for the benefit of all humankind.

Points and questions you may want to ponder:

What was the conflict in the story "It Is Just Business"?

Do you think conflict could have been dealt with differently?

Competition

> Competition occurs when two or more entities want something that cannot be shared as it is and oppose each other to acquire it. This activity results in a winner and a loser.

Just like many people across the world, I enjoy sports, and as you know, sports are often focused on winning. It is said that everyone loves a winner, and no one likes being a loser. Many sports are competitive. Every competitive sport requires the participants to do something to try to win. The person or group that does whatever is better than the other side wins, and the other side loses. One side leaves the competition happy, and the other side leaves sad. This difference in the participants' emotional state is based on gratification due to the perceived value of what the winners receive as a prize for winning. Winners have received positive reinforcement all their lives and have learned they get more of what they want when winning compared with when they lose. We know people feel better when they get what they want, at least in the short term.

I believe competition is good up to a point and can develop additional strength in a person if they do not lose too often. If they lose too often, there can be unanticipated consequences. Over my lifetime, I have observed the considerable emphasis placed on the importance of competition in this world. It seems the entertainment, sports industry, the media, and our education system have made idols of winners. Competing and playing to win are reenacted countless times across this world in families, businesses, and governments.

You may have noticed something is happening in which masses of people are developing negative attitudes because they are not winning enough. This has discouraged them to the point of withdrawing from mainstream society and acceptable societal norms of behavior. The threshold for emotional discomfort has changed significantly. There is less tolerance for emotional distress in the world today. Due to this fact, more people than ever before are opting out. When people opt out, they do not play by the rules anymore. They say to themselves, "Since I cannot win, then what does it matter."

Over time, this creates a substantial societal problem simply because it gets much harder to find anyone who wants to participate and be part of a possible losing team. I propose we consider being more collaborative and less competitive so we all can win more often. If we collectively do not find a solution to this problem soon, this lack of representation and diversity may lead to everyone losing!

Points and questions you may want to ponder:

How do you think competition affected the outcome in the story "It Is Just Business"?

Could there have been a win-win?

Life-Changing Learning Opportunities

Please pause for a moment and list some of your thoughts and feelings from what you have just experienced. After doing this, I recommend you write down the actions you will take to affect your future for the better. Do this based on what comes first to your mind after reading the story with its accompanying foundational human knowledge.

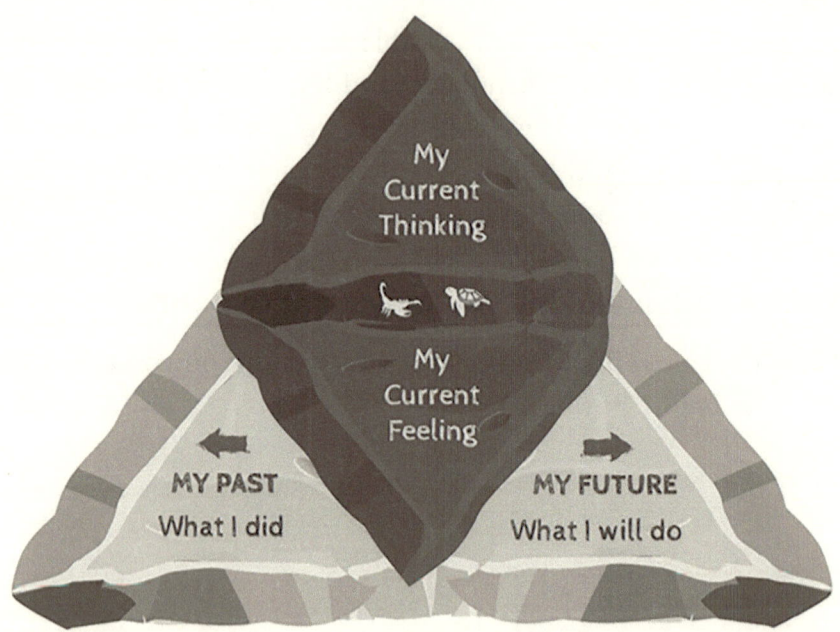

Figure 26: Life-Changing Learning Opportunities Pyramid

My Additional Current Thoughts

My Current Feelings

Actions That Will Affect My Future

Part III

Your Best Life

More Wisdom To Help You Survive Our Troubling Times

I have found many people know so much more about many other things than themselves and, as a result, often blame others for their unhappiness. If this is you, it can end today!

In the following chapters, you will learn more about how to have your best life. I hope you will take your time and think about what is shared with you.

CHAPTER EIGHTEEN

TAKING RESPONSIBILITY FOR YOUR LIFE

I know many of you are thinking, is taking responsibility for one's life even possible? Since we have gone this far together, we might as well go a little farther. It has been my experience that fewer and fewer people, are interested in taking responsibility for their life. Others want to but feel overwhelmed. I have found many people see this in an all-or-nothing way.[55] Either they assume complete responsibility or they take no responsibility at all for their life. I do not find this thinking helpful if one wants to survive our troubling times. I believe it is critical that each person take as much responsibility for their life as possible given the context in which they live. As you may have already guessed, I am not in favor of adopting a strategy of becoming completely powerless[56] and adopting a victim mentality[57] throughout one's life to survive unless there is no other option.

---

[55] Burns, D. D. (1999). Feeling Good: The New Mood Therapy. Harper Collins.
[56] Mack, J. (1994). Power, Powerlessness, and Empowerment in Psychotherapy. Psychiatry, 57(2), 178 -198. https://doi.org/10.1080/00332747.1994.11024684.
[57] Goens, G. A. (2017). It's Not My Fault: Victim Mentality and Becoming Response-able. Rowman & Littlefield.

It is easy to look at the world from the point of view of a passenger in a car who is taken for a ride. I have already shared that sometimes that it is good to go with the flow. Let me now add, it is crucial to pick your fights and not fight every battle as if it were the main war. That does not mean you are not responsible for your life. No matter how much of your life is difficult and challenging for you, giving up is not the answer!

When life is difficult, it simply means you have a choice to make; it is your life. Yes, it is your choice, not anyone else's. **You can make the deliberate choice to have the best life possible by taking responsibility for your life.** There is no way to get around that. If you choose not to choose, you most likely will not have the best life possible.

Have you noticed the swiftness at which things happen in this world currently? In my lifetime, I know there has been a great deal of technological change and other innovations that have affected the world we live in today. I will take this opportunity to point out some of these changes to present a point I will make afterward.

You already know I believe we are on this planet for a purpose at this given time in history. Each of us has been given certain personal assets and access to certain technologies to accomplish our purpose.

Here are but a few that have been made available in my lifetime. Feel free to make your own and add to my list.

- The computer mouse was invented[58]
- In healthcare, successful coronary bypass surgery was first performed in America[59]

---

[58] https://www.scientificamerican.com/article/origins-computer-mouse/.
[59] Bakaeen, F. G., Blackstone, E. H., Pettersson, G. B., Gillinov, A. M., & Svensson, L. G. (2018). The father of coronary artery bypass grafting: René Favaloro and the 50th anniversary of coronary artery bypass grafting. The Journal of Thoracic and Cardiovascular Surgery, 155(6), 2324–2328. https://doi.org/10.1016/j.jtcvs.2017.09.167.

- Apple II, Commodore PET, and Radio Shack's TRS-80 are the first PCs[60]
- Scanning tunneling microscope design earned IBM researchers a Nobel Prize[61]
- HTML is created to make Web pages to store information, and Uniform Resource Locators (URLs) to identify where it is stored[62]
- Wi-Fi became available to the masses[63]
- Sony released PlayStation [64]
- Apple's first iPhone[65]
- First Tesla all-electric Roadster car[66]
- President Donald Trump cleared the way to use all beneficial technologies to mitigate the consequences of the many COVID-19 virus variants[67]
- Artificial General Intelligence (AGI) - reinforcement learning without explicit instructions[68]

---

[60] Ethw. (2019, October 24). The First PCs - Engineering and Technology History Wiki. ETHW. https://ethw.org/The_First_PCs.
[61] The Nobel Prize in Physics 1986. NobelPrize.org. Nobel Prize Outreach 2025. Sun. 16 Feb 2025.
[62] webfoundation.org/about/vision/history-of-the-web/.
[63] https://www.nma.gov.au/defining-moments/resources/wi-fi.
[64] Britannica, The Editors of Encyclopaedia. "PlayStation". Encyclopedia Britannica, 9 Apr. 2024, https://www.britannica.com/ topic/PlayStation. Accessed 18 April 2024.
[65] time.com/4628515/steve-jobs-iphone-launch-keynote-2007/.
[66] https://www.energy.gov/timeline-history-electric-car.
[67] https://time.com/6146907/donald-trump-covid-19-vaccines-base/.
[68] Scott McLean, Gemma J. M. Read, Jason Thompson, Chris Baber, Neville A. Stanton & Paul M. Salmon (2023) The risks associated with Artificial General Intelligence: A systematic review, Journal of Experimental & Theoretical Artificial Intelligence, 35:5, 649-663, DOI: 10.1080/0952813X.2021.1964003.

You are now more aware of a few of the significant changes in technology and innovation that have occurred during many of our lifetimes. It is rather obvious that technology has had a profound effect on the society in which it operates. It does this by affecting and influencing what and how we learn, how we live, and how we use our most limited and precious resource, our time. Not long ago, it was IBM's prediction that the world's knowledge would be doubling every eleven to twelve hours.[69] Did you get your mind wrapped around that? This doubling will likely continue to be even faster in the future. "Poof!" That is the sound a brain makes when it does not know how to understand what it conceives.

Technology and world knowledge may be rapidly changing, but people's "core essence" has not. There have been turtle-like people and scorpion-like people among us since the early days of humanity. Just as change is constant, so is the need for each of us to look at our lives and use technology responsibly. Technology does not negate that we must take responsibility for our own lives and the decisions we make. I will talk more about this when I discuss a particular kind of artificial Intelligence later in this book. Think about that for a minute. Okay, a minute is up. Let us move on.

---

[69] futuristgerd.com/2014/07/knowledge-doubling-every-12-months-soon-to-be-every-12-hours-via-industry-tap/.

CHAPTER NINETEEN

REALITY CHECK

"Worlds within worlds." There are several books with those words in their titles. I have found none that have used this term and defined it how I intend to. I am defining these three words to mean each person on Earth exists and shares to some degree what makes up the Earth. Yet, each person has their own experiences based on their consciousness. What makes this possible? I think it has to do with the relationship between perception, reason, cause and effect, belief, and reality on the one hand versus the existence and recognition of truth on the other.

> **Worlds within Worlds**
> Each person on Earth exists and shares to some degree what makes up the Earth. Yet, each person has their own experiences based on their consciousness.

What is reality anyway? Have you ever heard someone say, "Perception is reality"?[70] I think it is helpful to explore where the belief in "perception is reality" comes from, what it means, and its limitations.

---

[70] onlinelibrary.wiley.com/doi/abs/10.1111/1745-9133.12036.

More than three decades ago, a politician by profession named Lee Atwater made the statement, "Perception is reality." This statement became popular in the 1980s in America. He created it out of the need for creative marketing during the George Bush campaign. Over the years, mainstream media picked it up. Some of you may be thinking that the statement "perception equals reality" is not the same as "perception is reality," or is it? Is that all there is? My answer to each question is the same. No, it is not.

We must each become fully awake to what is happing in this world. It seems many people are being used as pawns on a chessboard. We have become a means to an end. The ends can no longer justify the means. Governments can no longer be so separated from real life. Businesses can no longer be separated from real life. Governments and corporations are affecting real people's lives, which has a profound impact on the present and future all human beings. When will we accept the truth that all of us are many parts of one body?[71] We are all human beings. When are we going to become who we really are? It has been said, "A house divided cannot stand."[72]

We must redefine what winning means to us. We all win when we stand together for the betterment of humankind. We can no longer accept the statement: I win, and you lose. It must be a win for all of us, or we will all lose in the end. As I stated earlier, no one knows how many heartbeats they will have in life, and yes, the end is always closer than you think. Let us stop and examine ourselves before humankind is gone forever. Each of us plays a crucial role in the survival of us all.

You may be asking, "What world are you living in, Dr. Bill?" I am glad you asked. You will find my response in the next chapter.

---

[71] https://ebible.org/study/?v1=C112_1&t1=local%3Aeng-web&w1=bible.
[72] https://ebible.org/study/?v1=MT12_22&t1=local%3Aeng-web&w1=bible.

CHAPTER TWENTY

REAL-WORLD REALITY VERSUS VIRTUAL-WORLD REALITY

I hope it is okay if I get real with you. Not that I have not been real with you up to this point. I would not be who I am if I did not take on this important topic and provide you with some serious things to consider. I have previously shared with you that much of this book's content comes from many of my life experiences. In my practice as Dr. Bill, I draw from a mixture of "old school and new school" understanding.

I think it is time to look at the topic of real-world reality versus virtual-world reality. Let me begin with what I mean by real world reality. I define real-world reality as looking at and experiencing life as it really is, by using one of our five senses within the context of the natural world.

I believe we are now at a point in human history in which we are looking at two vastly different choices

> **Real-World Reality**
> I define *real-world reality* as looking at and experiencing life as it really is, by using one of our five senses within the context of the natural world.

as to how we will live. We can choose to live in a real-world reality or in a virtual-world reality. This is one of the most critical decisions each of us will have to make in our lifetime. Ultimately, the choice we make will determine the future of humankind.

A Real-World Reality and Why It Matters

Let's begin by looking at the choice of living in a real-world reality. To live in a real-world reality, one would have to agree that there is such a thing as real. There lies the problem. It is sometimes exceedingly difficult to discern what is real from what is not.

I have been a person who has enjoyed fine wristwatches. I learned early in my life that things of real quality are rare and cost more money than those that are not. This applies to wristwatches, as well as other things. When I look online, there are many brands and models of wristwatches from which to choose. Many of these wristwatch models look on the outside like authentic watches from a genuine manufacturer. It is not until one opens the watch's case and examines it that it becomes clear it is not a authentic watch from the original manufacturer, but a less valuable copy. I do not presume to speak for all wristwatch collectors. Still, I think it is safe to say none of them would feel particularly good about paying thousands of dollars for what they believe is a genuine wristwatch made by a well-known watch company, only to end up with a fake copy. I present this one example as concrete evidence that real exists and real matters.

Some of you might say, "I do not agree, and I am entitled to my opinion." I agree with you that you are entitled to your opinion, but that does not change the fact that there exists a real reality built on the foundation of truth.

You have just read or heard one example of the many benefits of choosing to live life in a real-world reality. This example points out one can avoid unnecessary pain if one is alert and takes appropriate action in a real-world reality. That said, a big disadvantage to living in a real-world reality is that you will be faced with real pain, which, if it does not destroy you, can make you a more capable, healthier, and happier human being. Not all pain is bad. It gives me no pleasure to tell you that pain is sometimes necessary for life to improve. It has been my experience that human beings can learn a great deal from pain. For me, the most significant benefit of pain is personal growth.

Let me state I am not into pain. I am just like most of you, and I would prefer to avoid unnecessary pain and pursue appropriate pleasure. I also know pain is often an indication for one's concern. If we do not address the pain we have within, we might not have a future. Living in a real-world reality is helpful for most of us because it enables us to identify the real problems in our lives and find real solutions. As human beings, these solutions can provide us with the real opportunity to move forward into a better future.

Over the years, there has been significant debate by scholars and philosophers concerning human beings and reality. In the eighteenth century, David Hume, a famous Scottish Enlightenment philosopher, historian, economist, and essayist, said, "We gather information through sight, smell, sound, touch, and taste."[73] Using this input, our brains automatically interpret the world around us and create the experience of what we call reality, but it is not real. Instead, it is just our perception of reality which makes all of us live in a virtual world all the time.[74]

---

[73] https://iep.utm.edu/hume-ima/.
[74] Gilliland, K., Humphreys. L., Good+Well, How Your Perception Is Your Reality, According to Psychologists, Feb 7, 2020.

Being human implies that your reality changes constantly. It appears our reality changes, whether we add reason to it or not. So, what happens if we do add conscious reasoning to it? In some situations, we can use this to our benefit. You may be familiar with something called *the placebo effect*. It involves the documented truth that the strength of a person's belief can alter real reality.[75] Let me give you an example of what I mean. There are numerous examples in medicine where the person is involved in an experimental, double-blind study and thinks they are receiving innovative treatment that will cure their terminal illness. As a result, their condition appears to be completely gone from their body in a relatively short period. They are unaware that they only received a common sugar pill as a placebo.[76] There are many other examples of how people's beliefs can change reality, such as when people think their physical work counts as exercise. This can dramatically accelerate their weight loss, and they do lose weight regardless of whether they exercise at work or not.[77] Most of us know that our bodies are capable of amazing things. In general, we get sick when our bodies cannot keep us well.

Virtual-World Reality

Now it's time to turn our attention to our second choice, to live in a Virtual-World Reality, which I will define as a reality intentionally created by manipulating the human brain, often through technology, using one or more of our five senses. It is a deliberately altered

---

[75] https://www.health.harvard.edu/mental-health/the-power-of-the-placebo-effect.
[76] Arnstein P, Broglio K, Wuhrman E, Kean MB (2011). "Use of placebos in pain management" (PDF). Pain Manag Nurs (Position Statement of the American Society for Pain Management Nursing). 12 (4): 225–9. doi:10.1016/j.pmn.2010.10.033. PMID 22117754.
[77] https://www.heart.org/en/healthy-living/fitness/fitness-basics/why-is-physical-activity-so-important-for-health-and-wellbeing.

reality. Computer engineers, psychologists, and others are creating virtual environments to create virtual world realities for people by using technologies such as VR that imitate real-life situations and provide a natural sense of immersion to the point of people having expected and predictable physiological reactions to what they are experiencing. With the aid of modern technology, these artificially created virtual-world realities have the potential to be of great help to humankind as well as one of its greatest threats. Earlier, I reminded that you there has been an enormous rise in technology in our lifetime here on Earth. None may affect all our futures as much as advancements in Artificial Intelligence (AI), supercomputers, and quantum computing. Consistent with this chapter's subject, I will point out one of these advancements, in AI that will involve Virtual Reality (VR). My definition of VR is as follows: The deliberate creation of an artificial environment with software and hardware designed to fool a person's brain through their senses into believing what they are experiencing is real.

> **Virtual Reality (VR)**
> The deliberate creation of an artificial environment with software and hardware designed to fool a person's brain through their senses into believing what they are experiencing is real.

Much of the purpose of VR is to immerse the person in an artificial world that the person can manipulate. It is simply creating the unreal, primarily made for getting one to accept the unreal as though it were real. Just a few years ago, it was estimated that 171 million people worldwide used VR. Most of the use is in the United States by males under thirty.[78] Please pause for a minute to get your head around what I just said. Can you think of any concerns this might raise for you as parents, given that the brains of your

---

[78] statista.com/statistics/740747/vr-ar-ownership-usa-gender/.

children may not yet be fully developed? What is happening as a result? Some of our children and college-age adults are developing and programming their brains into accepting VR as though it were real. Wow! This concerns many of the parents and academics I have discussed this with over my career.

In carrying out my work on this book, I read numerous articles on VR. One article caught my attention as it related to children. It was an article, featured on a well-known news network titled "The very real dangers of virtual reality." If you are interested, you can search for the article and read it in its entirety. Several times in the article, a researcher at Stanford and founding director of Stanford's Virtual Human Interaction Lab stated that "when VR is done well, the brain believes it is real." Do you know that VR is stored in the brain's memory center in ways that are strikingly like the way real-world physical experiences are stored? Have you looked at some of the VR games children and young adults are playing? Many are full of violence and sexual content. There are even games that show suicide, which I will not name, but I need you to know they are out there. I believe that given our brains cannot always tell the difference between what is real and what is not with this technology, I think it would not be a good idea to use it in ways you would not do in your regular life. VR produces greater changes in real-life attitudes and behavior than when watching videos or performing role-playing, from what I have read.

I hope from what I just shared. You can understand why VR is more than just entertainment; it is much more than that. There needs to be more research and longitudinal studies done on the effects of VR on children and their lifelong development up to and through adulthood.

Positive Benefits of VR in Life

I am an advocate of a balanced approach to living. Moderation is my view unless we are talking about chocolate ice cream. Yes, everyone has something to work on! In the interest of staying balanced, it is time to look at some of the benefits of VR and how it can improve our lives. VR is helping to save lives around the globe. VR is nothing short of revolutionary in training professionals in healthcare, aviation, the oil and gas industry, and elsewhere. In healthcare alone, this technology is improving patient care by increasing the surgeon's skills with simulations. For example, the University of British Columbia, Mayo Clinic, and Boston Shoulder Institute have created three types of simulation platforms for training surgeons worldwide in their work: the Trauma Platform, the Patient-Specific Anatomy Platform, and the Arthroplasty Platform.

This is ultimately making new treatment options possible with improved outcomes, which would have been unimaginable only a few years ago. VR is not only helping surgeons, but other physicians as well, through employing a whole range of other platforms that are being used in many hospitals, including Cincinnati Children's Hospital and Primary Children's Hospital to name only a few.[79]

All over the world, the population is getting older, and many seniors have limited mobility, often being homebound and alone for much of the time. There are studies now testing whether VR can improve the wellness and happiness of the aging members of our society. In fact, in a VR world, our brains experience and accept life as it is being presented; seniors using VR can go to exotic places and have virtual pets and friends without getting

---

[79] techopedia.com/how-virtual-reality-is-changing-healthcare/2/33891.

up. VR could even improve the significant problem of seniors feeling lonely.

I hope you can see that one does not have to be so limited because of one's circumstances, and instead can be anything and go anywhere in a virtual-world reality. There maybe a time soon when medications or other forms of force do not control human behavior, but varied forms of virtual reality are used instead? I am sure we are only at the beginning of our understanding of how VR is going to change our future.

I included this for you because I wanted to raise the awareness of parents and people worldwide to some of the uses of technology. Particularly how technology can deliberately or inadvertently create a society in the future that is less connected to a real-world reality based on truth. We are already seeing people trying to escape a real-world reality for many reasons.

I am genuinely concerned that if many in this world continue to move further and further away from a real-world reality, there is a high probability they may lose the best part of being a real human being. This is the part of us that cares not only for ourselves but also for others and our tiny, fragile planet. We are all this planet has, and it depends on us to be good stewards. I hope it is obvious to everyone that currently, when our planet is gone, so are all of us; that implies *game over*. Our entire survival depends on this planet! This world may not be perfect, but it is all each of us has, and I want to make the best of it. I hope you do, too.

You already know I believe one person can make a real difference, and together we can change the world. This is as true today as it was in Socrates' time. **I hope you now know that we must first turn our focus inward to examine ourselves before we can change the world for the better.**

CHAPTER TWENTY-ONE

A BRIEF MESSAGE TO TURTLE-LIKE PEOPLE

Are you primarily a turtle-like person? If so, you can stand tall! You possess some of the best qualities of humankind. You are not interested in hurting anyone, and you are a giver. There is an opportunity for you to take what you have learned in this unique self-improvement book and apply it to your life in a concrete way. I encourage you to open your mind to the real-world reality you are aware of now and not withdraw back into your shell.

Even though it is not in your nature to confront what is wrong, you must choose to do so not only for yourself, but also for your family and loved ones. You can be victorious if you stand up for yourself in the right way! That is the good news.

Now, here comes the bad news. If you are a turtle-like person, then you know more than ever that scorpion-like people surround you. So, what are you to do?

Forgive the analogy, but you know I like sports, and I recall watching a few boxing matches on TV with my grandfather earlier in my life. I remember there were two boxers and a referee, and part of the instructions the referee gave are truly relevant to you as a turtle-like person. The instruction I am talking about is when the two boxers are always told to keep their gloves up and defend themselves.

I am now going to give you some life-changing instructions I hope you will never forget! Be who you are. Never let your guard down all the way. Be ready to defend yourself if necessary! You can be successful in this world and have the life you always wanted without intentionally hurting others unnecessarily to get there.

> Be who you are. Never let your guard down all the way. Be ready to defend yourself if necessary! You can be successful in this world and have the life you always wanted without intentionally hurting others unnecessarily to get there.

That said, I would encourage you to learn all you can about scorpion-like people. Your very life could depend on it! This book may be a real revelation for you. I congratulate you on having begun to learn more about yourself and this world by experiencing and understanding the foundational human knowledge that this unique self-improvement book has offered to you.

You are now on your way to having the best life possible. You must continue making a stand and choosing to live based on what you know rather than only what you think or feel. I hope and pray you will choose to live in a real-world reality where *Truth* still matters!

CHAPTER TWENTY-TWO

A BRIEF MESSAGE TO SCORPION-LIKE PEOPLE

I wonder what you might be thinking right now. Let me tell you what I am thinking. First, I want you to know that I am not here to judge or condemn you. If you have taken the time to read or listen this far in the book, you might be asking yourself, "Is primarily being a scorpion-like person in survival mode all the time the only way to live or even the best way?" I hope you are thinking in that direction. If you are not, I would ask you to consider it now. Since this message is for you, I am only thinking of you at this moment. How much better could life be if you to allowed the past to stay in the past? I believe if you know and accept the truth; it will set you free.[80]

If you understand and believe in *Truth*, you already know your value cannot come from your power, how many people you control, your parents, the color of your skin, country of origin, educational level, or how much money you acquire on Earth. Your value as a human being is the same as mine and every other

---

[80] https://ebible.org/study/?w1=bible&t1=local%3Aeng-web&v1=JN8_32.

> **Within you is something no one else has. You are special! I would challenge you to be who you were made to be, You are intended to be a protector and a compassionate leader of others, and a loving human being.**

human being's. You have great value, and your value is given to you at birth, as it was to me. I believe you are a wonderful creation, the highest life form on planet Earth, and exceedingly rare. You are a one-of-one.

Within you is something no one else has. You are special! I would challenge you to be who you were made to be. You are intended to be a protector and a compassionate leader of others, and a loving human being. I know the anger you have is not helping you. Science and medicine tell us that anger and high stress levels are the destroyers of our health.[81] When is enough *enough*? Do you really need any more pain? It does not matter if you can take it. What matters is that you are missing a lot of what life has to offer. I mean, the good stuff!

To experience the best of life, you do not need more pain, hurt and anger, but more positives, like real love. I am not talking about what you can get but what you can give to another person. Real love is when you are primarily in the relationship to give, not just to get your wants met. You must allow yourself to get out of survival mode. There can be so much more to life than just survival. I have said it before: you must survive, but you do not have to stop there. It is so important you move on to what this life is really about. I am talking about a genuine and safe connection to a loving human being.

Please allow me to share an experience that changed my life for the better. Time seems to go by so fast. It was almost twenty years ago when I had the opportunity to do some consulting

---

[81] hms.harvard.edu/magazine/science-emotion/anger-management.

work with three nursing homes. I had not spent much time in a nursing home other than with a few family members who were in different ones briefly. I remember my experiences in these nursing homes as though they were just last week. I expected to see the very old, and I did, but I did not expect to see people in their thirties and forties who were burned out due to substance abuse and living a lifestyle that was just too much for their brains and bodies to heal from.

After a few weeks of work in the nursing homes, I began to feel more at ease with what I saw, heard, and smelled. There were times when I would talk to a resident in the morning, and they would die the next day. Many of the residents in the nursing homes I spoke to had been there for months. At some point in my time there, I found the courage to ask a personal question I had wanted to ask for weeks. I was respectful of each of them and asked if it was okay to ask this personal question beforehand. The question I began asking the nursing home residents was the following: "When you reflect on your life, what would you say means the most to you? In other words, to put the question more clearly, what has been the absolute best part of having a life?" Every single person was eager to share their answer with me. I asked over a hundred people the same question.

Before asking this question, I assumed I would get answers such as *I enjoyed having a house on the beach. I liked being the CEO of a top 100 company,* and *I am glad I had a hospital named after me.* To my greatest surprise, the number-one answer I received from my question touched my heart in a way that changed me forever!

The answer came in the form of two sentences. Their response was, "I am happy to tell you what has mattered to me the most. What has meant the most for me was the people I loved and the people who loved me." To my delight, I learned an extraordinary life lesson from these kind people who had just hours to live in some cases. I learned from them that amid all the important things in life, interacting with people lovingly matters the most!

This interaction is not one of selfishness but rather one of selflessness. It is a life based on quality, not just quantity. It is a life well-lived because you choose to be open and real by allowing others to love you! You do not have to be "perfect" or to be what others want you to be. Just be the absolute best you can be. Life can be tough, but each of us has a choice not to give up on ourselves or humanity's future. You do not have anything to prove. You are already somebody! You can choose to love and to be loved. You can choose to be transformed by the renewing of your mind.[82] I promise you, if you do your life will never be the same. I know you are a fighter and a survivor. **I am just asking you to fight for something worth fighting for, the real you!**

---

[82] https://ebible.org/study/?w1=bible&t1=local%3Aeng-web&v1=RM12_2.

CHAPTER TWENTY-THREE

BONUS: BEING VERSUS DOING

Doing is different from being. *Being* is the only state of existence in which you can take responsibility for what you are doing. When somebody asks you to introduce yourself, and you say you are a mom, dad, nurse, teacher, or firefighter, soldier, world-class athlete, entertainer, or businessperson, you are talking about what you do, not who you are. There seems to be a fair amount of confusion among many people as to the differences.

For example, if you take me, some might see me as a scholar and writer. I have written over 28 books, earned six college degrees, including a master's and doctorate, and counseled, coached and mentored people from all walks of life as a business leader and behavioral health professional and provided consulting to business and government entities, but who I am is more than that. I designed and built a September 11th Freedom Memorial, an 18-foot water sculpture made from stainless steel and concrete, but that does not make me only an artist or sculptor. I am more than just that. I am suggesting that, like me, you are much more than just what you do or have done. Each of us has an opportunity during our lives to find out who we really are. I believe each of us is a unique creation with a purpose given to us at birth to fulfill during our lives. Do not get me wrong. It is clear to me that we need doers because there would be no being without doing. There has been a great deal of doing during the last two hundred years, and some of this doing has created pain for many individuals in this world. I wonder, when are we going to focus our attention on learning how to live our lives more fully without hurting others? When will we understand and value the gift of being alive to the fullest? For me, living a quality life is about being authentic and being who we really are, not just what we want the world to see and believe we are.

Have you ever thought about why many people are in such a hurry in life? For what? In other words, why not learn to enjoy the process of life as much as the destination. Think about it. How hard is it for you to keep your mind still and quiet? Many people are completely uncomfortable with silence. They must always be busy doing one thing or another. If this is you, I would again ask you to consider the possibility that life is more than just doing; it is also about being. Be who you are designed to be. If you decide to slow down your doing and discover who you are designed to be, it can be a real game-changer for you and your family. If you are primarily a doer, this concept may seem somewhat foreign to you.

I am not talking about just the quantity of life; I am talking about the quality of life. I am aware that many people believe that quantity and quality are the same; they think that more is always better. If that were the case, more and more pain in life would always be better. That is just not true, is it? Many people believe there is only one way to be a doer: you must take what you want. I want; therefore, I am going to get mine. After all, no one gives you anything. This is a common worldview, which is encouraged and taught by scorpion-like leaders.

This is a view based on survival at all cost. It is about power and control. I know the world we live in currently requires many people to live this way to survive because we have non-transformed scorpion-like people in all countries. I would ask you to consider that people make countries, and those people have a lot to do with how scorpion-like people in those countries behave.

I believe people are adaptive, and if they do not need to act or be a certain way, many will choose a different path. I am under no illusion that some people are predators, and we must always protect ourselves from being predators' prey.

I hope by now you have begun to examine your life and think more about the life you want for yourself and your family in the future. I implore you to choose not to let the ends justify the means and work with others to support and encourage them. This world can only be different if we all choose to interact with the common goal of a win-win situation, which means nobody must continually lose in the future. I believe you want to have a life well-lived, as most of us do. **I have found that if you do not understand who you are, it makes the doing part of life more complicated and a lot more painful.** I hope you better understand now that before any of us *do* anything, we must *discover* who we were designed to be. We must strive to be the best we can be. Then and only then can we effectively do much to help ourselves, our loved ones, and this world.

EPILOGUE

Much of my education has focused on helping people learn how to survive and to thrive in their societies. My work as a professional psychotherapist, life coach and executive coach, and business leader has allowed me to engage with thousands of individuals from many cultures and countries around the world.

There is a foundation on which much of my clinical training has been built. It is abnormal psychology and social psychology. The basic premise is that people need help because they have problems coping with life for a multitude of reasons. Some reasons are biological, and some are environmental. There can be little doubt that people can and do break down physically, mentally, emotionally, and even spiritually from being who they are, interacting within their society, and coping with their life circumstances. However, I think not all suffering people suffer from well-known mental health disorders such as depression, anxiety, PTSD, stress, dissociative disorders, ED, ADD, or OCD, but from what I believe is a *world fatigue syndrome*.

I define **world fatigue syndrome** as:

> **World Fatigue Syndrome** is the toxicity of the world exceeding an individual's capacity to filter it out and be fully functioning in life.

It is evidenced by a significant and persistent breakdown in one's physical, mental, emotional, and spiritual health. People experiencing this syndrome cannot reintegrate and maintain balance using healthy coping mechanisms without appropriate support.

> A. In the beginning stages:
> — A person may not care about others. Individuals not only see themselves as being victimized, but they may believe they are a victim for life.
> — Therefore, they feel entitled to do or not to do whatever they want, no matter the adverse effects on others.
>
> B. In the later stages:
> — Individuals may lose all hope, become apathetic, and no longer care about themselves and this planet.

There is one perplexing question I still have after all these years:

> Is it **abnormal** to have problems when the society one lives in is in **crisis** and extremely **dysfunctional**?

Stated another way:

> Is it normal for a **sane** person to have problems in an **insane** world?

Previously, in this self-improvement book, beginning with the original fable of the scorpion and the turtle, I introduced you to two primary sides of people. I went on to illuminate how they may have been created and made, how each one is different, how to recognize them, and how each can change over time. You have also been given information about why you need to know what a foundational law is, as well as essential foundational human knowledge to be wiser and to survive our troubling times.

It is, however, up to you as to what you do with this information and your new understanding. I pray you will use your knowledge responsibly to enhance the quality of your life and your loved ones' lives, thus leaving this world better than you found it! I hope you will agree that your future and your personal life choices matter. With so much going on in life and changes occurring so quickly and frequently, I can see why many people throw up their hands and give up on having much control over their lives. This creates a lot of apathy, and many people have completely lost confidence in themselves, others, and their governments.

That said, as I stated earlier, personal life choices matter, and so do all our futures. A scorpion-like person once told me, "You are a survivor!" This was just before I experienced what scorpion-like people can do. I am here today, so they were right, and I am here today to say to you that surviving is especially important, but it is not all there is! I am, without question, a survivor, and you are too, or you would not be reading or hearing this book now.

Certainly, I know you must do all that you can sometimes, just to survive, and there is no shame in that. Although significant challenges are often a part of our life journey, it does not have to be our destination, as many scorpion-like people intend it to be.

Over the years, many people have come to me for help with their most difficult life challenges and situations. They have read many books, including marriage books and focused couples books. They find themselves dealing with some of the negatives of being a human being in contact with other human beings. This challenge, known as "a relationship," is unavoidable. They have been hurt, often betrayed, and never saw it coming. Almost weekly I get questions like, "How could they do this to our children or me." It appears they have taken the victim position and are looking for ways to survive what has happened. I do all that I can to help them understand that even though they may have been victimized, they will heal faster by not accepting being a victim. I work with them through the challenges because I want them to benefit, not just by surviving but by thriving!

You might be saying, "But, Dr. Bill, you have not been through what I have. You do not understand how painful this is. How hard it is for me." You are right, I do not, and neither does anyone else. I believe your pain and how you feel belongs to you. No one can make you feel. Your feelings are your feelings, right? Right! Since we agree that your feelings reside in you, and they are yours and yours alone, we can now move from just surviving to a much better place of thriving! As people, we cannot be in two places at once. We are in either survival mode or thriving mode, but not at the same time. Which would you rather be in?

It may be hard to believe, but for some people, there are reasons they may want to stay in survival mode and may never get past being victimized by a scorpion-like person. Whereas others find a way to survive and move on as quickly as possible to a better place of thriving.

You might be asking yourself, "How can I do that?" I am so glad you asked. Life can be better than you may be able to imagine. To get there, it helps to live intentionally and deliberately by being consciously awake, operating in the "real world," and putting into practice what you have been learning in this book. This will give you a better opportunity to live your best life, no matter what! I am confident you have already begun your journey to having the best life possible by reading or hearing this unique self-improvement book that I have designed to help you in your life's journey. I also know this may not be all you need.

I am including information on how to contact me directly if you choose. You can contact me through my website:

https://SingerInstitute.com

… to schedule a personal appointment for individual counseling, marriage counseling, couples counseling, coaching by phone, or video. If you would like, you can sign up for online *SCORPIONS AND TURTLES* virtual groups at my website, where I will go deeper than the material in this unique book. The *SCORPIONS AND TURTLES Coaching Companion* workbook and journal, in addition to the thirteen personal workbooks and thirteen guided journals are designed to be used with the thirteen virtual groups or purchased to use as you choose. I am also available for consulting activities for governments, businesses, public speaking, and business retreats.

I am now inviting you to be a part of our *SCORPIONS AND TURTLES* community. Please join us for your healing and to help heal the world!

 **Facebook:** Scorpions And Turtles

 **Instagram:** Scorpions And Turtles

LinkedIn: Dr Bill Singer

Pinterest: Dr Bill Singer

X: @ScorpionDrBill

YouTube Channel: @Scorpions And Turtles

Special Request from the Author:

I intentionally wrote this book for you! To that end, I would appreciate it if you would consider leaving a review to encourage others by sharing how this unique self-improvement book has helped you. Please feel free to email me at:

DrBillSinger@SingerInstitute.com

… and let me know if some of what I have offered you in this book has been helpful. You never know—your email may inspire me to write additional books. Either way, I want to thank you for taking the time to experience my offering of *SCORPIONS AND TURTLES How To Survive Our Troubling Times*.

If you are a licensed behavioral health professional in the United States or hold the equivalent credentials in another country, you may be eligible to apply to become a *Scorpions and Turtles Coach*™. You can contact me with your request using the email provided above.

ACKNOWLEDGMENTS

I want to acknowledge The Great I AM, who has made all things, including this unique self-improvement book, possible! Then, I want to thank Diane, who one day said to me, "You ought to write a book," and for her assistance and belief in the importance of this book's topic. You are indeed a gift from God. Finally, I want to thank my high school English teacher at Lake Weir High School, who encouraged me to put more effort into her class. In retrospect, I should have listened to her even more.

ABOUT THE AUTHOR

Bill Singer, Psy.D., M.S.W., L.C.S.W., C.A.P., believes in doing as much as he can to make the world a better place. He is a lifelong learner and has earned six college degrees in the fields of psychology, sociology, and clinical social work. He is licensed in Florida as a psychotherapist and certified as an addiction professional. He is also certified as a master life coach, and an executive coach. In the last thirty-five years, his work in counseling, coaching, and the business world has provided him an exciting career.

He has led large healthcare organizations, including the day-to-day operational oversight of multi-million-dollar budgets and hundreds of employees. He has also directed health and social programs, serving thousands of children and families annually. For many decades in his private practice, he has enjoyed working with individuals, couples, and families. People come from all over the world and from C-suites who are professionals of for-profit and not-for-profit large and small companies, healthcare, religious and spiritual leadership, education, state and federal employees, the entertainment industry, and professional athletes to meet with Dr. Bill.

As a psychotherapist, and an executive and life coach, Dr. Bill is always interactive and solution-focused with his clients. His therapeutic approach provides supportive and practical feedback to help clients effectively address personal life challenges. He integrates unique complementary methodologies and techniques to offer a highly personalized approach tailored to each client. He is committed to working with individuals and couples to help them build on their strengths and obtain the life they always wanted. For Dr. Bill, it is not just about surviving life. It is all about helping people reach their full potential.

Regardless of who Dr. Bill is working with, he possesses the uncanny ability to understand and find unique, real-world solutions to help that person or couple reach their maximum potential. He is a sought-out management consultant, speaker, counselor, life coach, and executive coach, speaking on several topics. In 2007, he was published in the prestigious *Journal of The Joint Commission on Quality and Patient Safety*. That same year, while working as a healthcare operations manager, a program under his leadership was the only hospital program in the nation to be recognized for excellence and to receive the Ernest A. Codman National Hospital Quality Award by The Joint Commission.

APPENDICES

Glossary of Definitions of Each Foundational Human Knowledge

Foundational Human Knowledge List *(alphabetical order):*	Foundational Human Knowledge Definitions: *(Number of the companion Scorpions and Turtles' Virtual Group, Workbook & Journal)*	Page No.
Addiction	A connection to something or someone you cannot stop voluntarily, no matter the consequences. (No. 3)	65
Attachment	It is the emotional and psychological bond that often forms between a child and who cares for it. It helps children get their primary needs met. It can be a strong connection to places and things as well as ideas and beliefs. (No. 10)	185
Awareness	Knowing what is happening constitutes awareness. (No. 5)	102

Foundational Human Knowledge List *(alphabetical order):*	Foundational Human Knowledge Definitions: *(Number of the companion Scorpions and Turtles' Virtual Group, Workbook & Journal)*	Page No.
Beliefs	Core thoughts people have concerning truth that drives their behavior. (No. 4)	83
Change	To modify or make different. (No. 5)	96
Commitment	It means I will, or I will not, period. When you make a commitment, it means you must dedicate yourself to something or someone. (No. 10)	182
Communication	The method people use to express themselves to others; it most often involves writing, speaking, touch, and using body language. (No. 4)	85
Competition	It occurs when two or more entities want something that cannot be shared as it is and oppose each other to acquire it. This activity results in a winner and a loser. (No. 13)	242
Conflict	It is the natural and inevitable discord that occurs between unique human beings and within one's self. (No. 13)	240

Foundational Human Knowledge List *(alphabetical order):*	Foundational Human Knowledge Definitions: *(Number of the companion Scorpions and Turtles' Virtual Group, Workbook & Journal)*	Page No.
Cooperation	An action a person takes to work together for the good of themselves and others. (No. 10)	176
Denial	The most common mental state human beings' function in when they are in survival mode. It is designed to buy time for a person to process the truth that can be overwhelming in the moment while they try to manage in a complex world. (No. 7)	128
Dependence	An absolute connection of a person to another person, group, government, place, or thing for perceived survival. (No. 12)	217
Disappointment	The negative thought and feeling that results when a person gets less than they wanted or expected. (No. 1)	40
Doing	The process of taking action. (No. 8)	143
Dying	The process of losing a life. It results in no longer having a heartbeat and leads to death. (No. 3)	73
Emotion	It is the way in which humans ultimately experience life by perceiving something as positive or negative through their feelings. (No. 9)	160

Foundational Human Knowledge List *(alphabetical order)*:	Foundational Human Knowledge Definitions: *(Number of the companion Scorpions and Turtles' Virtual Group, Workbook & Journal)*	Page No.
Empathy	It is imagining what others may be going through mentally and emotionally by putting yourself in their place. (No. 8)	150
Expectations	Specific thoughts one has about how life should be. It is that which helps us know more, because we seek greater understanding. (No. 4)	81
Fear	A natural result of being afraid of something or of thinking that something undesirable might happen. We use it to alert ourselves to a potential threat to our well-being and survival. (No. 2)	54
Focus	The process by which people eliminate extraneous variables to take possible actions because of their interests and perceived importance. (No. 11)	203
Free Will	Having the freedom to choose one's actions from available possibilities. (No. 9)	158
Future	It is the time yet to happen. It is an unknown part of time, and it has no guarantees. (No. 6)	115
Grief	A painful human reaction, that often accompanies loss. The bigger the loss, the more likely one will experience grief. (No. 3)	70

Foundational Human Knowledge List (alphabetical order):	Foundational Human Knowledge Definitions: (Number of the companion Scorpions and Turtles' Virtual Group, Workbook & Journal)	Page No.
Habits	Repetitive thoughts, feelings, and behaviors that become internalized and automatic. (No. 4)	87
Hate	An extremely negative emotion based on one or more feelings generated from thoughts such as dislike and contempt, often with anger, which creates beliefs that are the opposite of love. (No. 9)	163
Human Brain	The part of a human being that directs the rest of the human body and is responsible for our thoughts, sensations, feelings, and actions. (No. 11)	198
Human Evolution	Is the biological connection human beings have to past generations, designed to help the species improve and adjust better to their current environment and continue to survive. (No. 11)	206
Human Footprint	The effect human beings are having and have had on themselves and this planet. (No. 9)	165
Impulse Control	The act of decreasing one's automatic responses to the environment by increasing the activation of the human brain's executive center. It allows for more logical deliberation and action. (No. 12)	219

Foundational Human Knowledge List *(alphabetical order)*:	Foundational Human Knowledge Definitions: *(Number of the companion Scorpions and Turtles' Virtual Group, Workbook & Journal)*	Page No.
Independence	The ability to choose for oneself, as demonstrated by selecting and acting on options, without being forced. (No. 5)	98
Insight	It is a state of mind that results in a more accurate understanding of what is. Insight is that which helps us know more because we seek greater understanding. (No. 5)	100
Instincts	The innate set of possible reactions used by people to survive and are chosen automatically by one's brain. (No. 8)	145
Intention	The why and what that is responsible for and occurs before all human action. It is one's reason for acting. (No. 1)	31
Interdependence	A state of being that involves being connected with something. The wellbeing of each depends on this connection to function well. (No. 12)	215
Justification	A commonly used reason people create and accept to explain their actions being right or just. (No. 7)	134
Leadership	A position one holds and actions one takes that involve power and influence over people. (No. 13)	237

Foundational Human Knowledge List (alphabetical order):	Foundational Human Knowledge Definitions: (Number of the companion Scorpions and Turtles' Virtual Group, Workbook & Journal)	Page No.
Learning	The obtaining of skills and knowledge by personal experience through one's study and from others' teachings. (No. 7)	131
Living	The minimal requirements to be alive, such as brain function, heartbeat, and other body functions necessary for life. Living is a choice to act and the action one takes to get the most out of being alive by maximizing life opportunities and personal assets. (No. 2)	57
Loss	What one experiences from not winning or from having something that is valued taken away and it almost always includes emotional pain. (No. 3)	68
Love	An extremely positive thought, feeling, or action designed to enhance human beings and bring them together to help one another and, in some cases, have children. Love is not just a thought or feeling but is demonstrable. (No. 2)	52
Magical Thinking	It is the unrealistic belief in what creates positive or negative outcomes based on something other than truth. (No. 10)	179

Foundational Human Knowledge List *(alphabetical order)*:	Foundational Human Knowledge Definitions: *(Number of the companion Scorpions and Turtles' Virtual Group, Workbook & Journal)*	Page No.
Motivation	It is what is required for people to act and is like an inner voice saying, "What's in it for me?" The motivation of a person, group, or nation is not constant but changes over time. This is often dependent on both the intention and the situation, including resource availability and timing. (No. 1)	36
Passivity	The lack of taking action—no matter what—when others do something that affects you. (No. 8)	148
Past	The part of time that has already occurred. (No. 6)	113
Present	The current part of time which is now. (No. 6)	111
Self-Acceptance	Being at peace with who you perceive yourself to be. (No. 12)	223
Situations	The context within which we exist and experience life as human beings. They occur throughout our lifetime. (No. 6)	118
Survival	The built-in need for and the attempt to continue to participate in life for one's own sake and for future generations. (No. 2)	50

Foundational Human Knowledge List *(alphabetical order)*:	Foundational Human Knowledge Definitions: *(Number of the companion Scorpions and Turtles' Virtual Group, Workbook & Journal)*	Page No.
Talent	A unique ability or abilities inherent in each of us from birth to be used to help us be naturally successful at some things without being taught. (No. 13)	234
Thinking	A mental process used to improve one's understanding of something in an attempt to make sense of the world. (No. 10)	196
Trust	An inherent requirement of human beings to take calculated risks with people. The more one trusts, the more chances one is able and willing to take with others. Fully trusting is the desirable state in which people strive to feel most comfortable with others and their environment. (No. 1)	34
Truth	That for which we seek, which does not change based on opinion, and is real in this world. (No. 7)	130

CHAPTER REVIEW PLANS

Foundational Human Knowledge Review Plan: Over Three (3) Months

Weekly Review Plan:	Chapter Numbers*:	Chapter Titles*:	13-Weeks Review Plan, with their four corresponding Foundational Human Knowledge examples:	Your review plan & progress:
Week 1	5	Is It Just Sibling Rivalry?	Pages 27-46	
Week 2	6	Love Finds a Way	Pages 47-60	
Week 3	7	Addiction and Relationships Don't Mix	Pages 61-76	
Week 4	8	It's Never Enough	Pages 77-91	
Week 5	9	What About Me?	Pages 93-106	

Weekly Review Plan:	Chapter Numbers*:	Chapter Titles*:	13-Weeks Review Plan, with their four corresponding Foundational Human Knowledge examples:	Your review plan & progress:
Week 6	10	Good Decision or Not?	Pages 107-121	
Week 7	11	It's a Secret	Pages 123-137	
Week 8	12	It's All About the Money	Pages 139-153	
Week 9	13	A One-Way Ticket	Pages 155-169	
Week 10	14	Death and Divorce	Page 171-189	
Week 11	15	Very Special Indeed	Pages 191-210	
Week 12	16	Finding Your Way	Pages 211-226	
Week 13	17	Welcome to the Real World	Pages 227-245	

Table 12: Chapter Review Plan in Three Months

SCORPIONS AND TURTLES How To Survive Our Troubling Times original book page numbers

Foundational Human Knowledge Review Plan: Over A Year

Note the date you plan to review this aspect of Foundational Human Knowledge in the fourth column. You may choose to put a checkmark "✓" in this column when your review is complete.

Weekly Review Plan	Each Chapter's Foundational Human Knowledge	One Year (fifty-two weeks)	Your Review Plan and Progress
Chapter Five*—Is It Just Sibling Rivalry?			
Week 1	☐ Intention	Pg. 31*	
Week 2	☐ Trust	Pg. 34*	
Week 3	☐ Motivation	Pg. 36*	
Week 4	☐ Disappointment	Pg. 40*	
Chapter Six*—Love Finds a Way			
Week 5	☐ Survival	Pg. 50*	
Week 6	☐ Love	Pg. 52*	
Week 7	☐ Fear	Pg. 54*	
Week 8	☐ Living	Pg. 57*	
Chapter Seven*—Addiction and Relationships Don't Mix			
Week 9	☐ Addiction	Pg. 65*	
Week 10	☐ Loss	Pg. 68*	
Week 11	☐ Grief	Pg. 70*	
Week 12	☐ Dying	Pg. 73*	
Chapter Eight*—It's Never Enough			
Week 13	☐ Expectations	Pg. 81*	
Week 14	☐ Beliefs	Pg. 83*	
Week 15	☐ Communication	Pg. 85*	

Weekly Review Plan	Each Chapter's Foundational Human Knowledge	One Year (fifty-two weeks)	Your Review Plan and Progress
Week 16	☐ Habits	Pg. 87*	
Chapter Nine*—What About Me?			
Week 17	☐ Change	Pg. 96*	
Week 18	☐ Independence	Pg. 98*	
Week 19	☐ Insight	Pg. 100*	
Week 20	☐ Awareness	Pg. 102*	
Chapter Ten*—Good Decision or Not?			
Week 21	☐ Present	Pg. 111*	
Week 22	☐ Past	Pg. 113*	
Week 23	☐ Future	Pg. 115*	
Week 24	☐ Situations	Pg. 118*	
Chapter Eleven*—It's a Secret			
Week 25	☐ Denial	Pg. 128*	
Week 26	☐ Truth	Pg. 130*	
Week 27	☐ Learning	Pg. 131*	
Week 28	☐ Justification	Pg. 134*	
Chapter Twelve*—It's All About the Money			
Week 29	☐ Doing	Pg. 143*	
Week 30	☐ Instincts	Pg. 145*	
Week 31	☐ Passivity	Pg. 148*	
Week 32	☐ Empathy	Pg. 150*	
Chapter Thirteen*—A One-Way Ticket			
Week 33	☐ Free Will	Pg. 158*	
Week 34	☐ Emotion	Pg. 160*	
Week 35	☐ Hate	Pg. 163*	

Chapter Review Plans 303

Weekly Review Plan	Each Chapter's Foundational Human Knowledge	One Year (fifty-two weeks)	Your Review Plan and Progress
Week 36	☐ Human Footprint	Pg. 165*	
Chapter Fourteen*—Death and Divorce			
Week 37	☐ Cooperation	Pg. 176*	
Week 38	☐ Magical Thinking	Pg. 179*	
Week 39	☐ Commitment	Pg. 182*	
Week 40	☐ Attachment	Pg. 185*	
Chapter Fifteen*—Very Special Indeed			
Week 41	☐ Thinking	Pg. 196*	
Week 42	☐ Human Brain	Pg. 198*	
Week 43	☐ Focus	Pg. 203*	
Week 44	☐ Human Evolution	Pg. 206*	
Chapter Sixteen*—Finding Your Way			
Week 45	☐ Interdependence	Pg. 215*	
Week 46	☐ Dependence	Pg. 217*	
Week 47	☐ Impulse Control	Pg. 219*	
Week 48	☐ Self-Acceptance	Pg. 223*	
Chapter Seventeen*—Welcome to the Real World			
Week 49	☐ Talent	Pg. 234*	
Week 50	☐ Leadership	Pg. 237*	
Week 51	☐ Conflict	Pg. 240*	
Week 52	☐ Competition	Pg. 242*	

Table 13: Foundational Human Knowledge Review Plan in One Year

* *SCORPIONS AND TURTLES How To Survive Our Troubling Times* original book page numbers

FOUNDATIONAL HUMAN KNOWLEDGE LIST

Check (√) off the individual foundational human knowledge when you are comfortable that you have learned it and can use it effectively to enhance your life.

Addiction	Doing	Human Evolution	Love
Attachment	Dying	Human Footprint	Magical Thinking
Awareness	Emotion	Impulse Control	Motivation
Beliefs	Empathy	Independence	Passivity
Change	Expectations	Insight	Past
Commitment	Fear	Instincts	Present
Communication	Focus	Intention	Self-Acceptance
Competition	Free Will	Interdependence	Situations
Conflict	Future	Justification	Survival
Cooperation	Grief	Leadership	Talent
Denial	Habits	Learning	Thinking
Dependence	Hate	Living	Trust
Disappointment	Human Brain	Loss	Truth

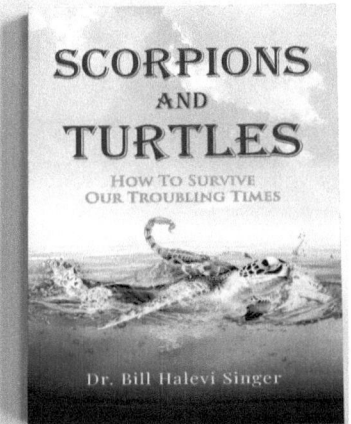

To enhance your life, read or listen to:
- A. Book
- B. Coaching Companion Workbook
- C. Personal Workbooks #1 - #13 & Personal Journals #1 - #13

In addition, there are 13 virtual groups.

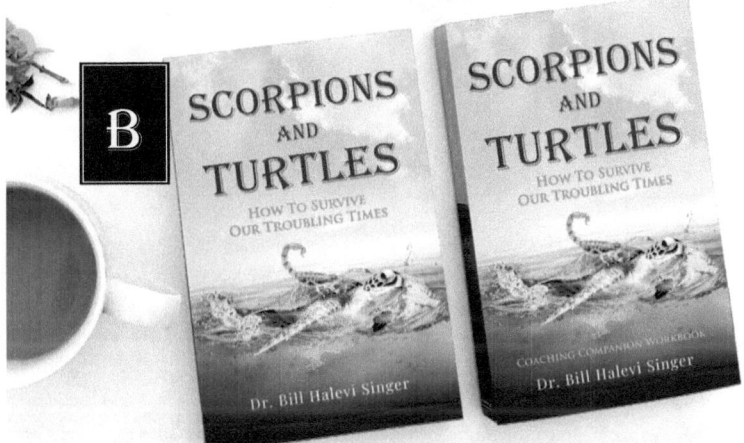

Always available from:
www.SingerInstitute.com
(QR scan code below) are:
-All the *SCORPIONS AND TURTLES* books, workbooks, & journals.
Exclusively at
www.SingerInstitute.com are the:
-*SCORPIONS AND TURTLES Virtual Groups (#1- #13).*

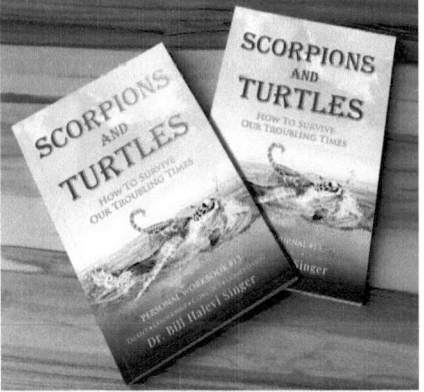

Formats available: Print- book, workbooks, & journals, **ebook-** book, workbooks, and journals.

Three ways to experience Dr. Singer's groundbreaking
**SCORPIONS AND TURTLES
How To Survive Our Troubling Times** book!

1. Paperback

2. ebook

3. Audiobook

www.SingerInstitute.com

Scorpions and Turtles Virtual Groups #1-#13 exclusively at >

www.ingramcontent.com/pod-product-compliance
Lightning Source LLC
Chambersburg PA
CBHW060550080526
44585CB00013B/512